COMMUNITIES
THAT CARE

J. David Hawkins
Richard F. Catalano, Jr.
and Associates

COMMUNITIES THAT CARE

*Action for
Drug Abuse
Prevention*

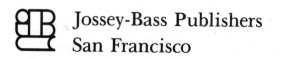
Jossey-Bass Publishers
San Francisco

For international orders, please contact your local Paramount Publishing International office.

The paper used in this book is acid-free and meets the State of California requirements for recycled paper (50 percent recycled waste, including 10 percent postconsumer waste), which are the strictest guidelines for recycled paper currently in use in the United States.

Library of Congress Cataloging-in-Publication Data

Hawkins, J. David.
    Communities that care : action for drug abuse prevention / J. David Hawkins, Richard F. Catalano, Jr., and associates. — 1st ed.
      p.   cm. — (A Joint publication of the Jossey-Bass social and behavioral science series and the Jossey-Bass education series)
    Includes bibliographical references (p.   ) and index.
    ISBN 1-55542-471-6 (acid-free)
    1. Drug abuse—United States—Prevention. 2. Alcoholism—United States—Prevention. I. Catalano, Richard F. II. Title.
III. Series: Jossey-Bass social and behavioral science series.
IV. Series: Jossey-Bass education series.
HV5825.H278 1992
364.1'77'0973—dc20
                                 92-11010
                                     CIP

FIRST EDITION
HB Printing   10 9 8 7 6 5 4 3 2   *Code 9268*

A joint publication of
the Jossey-Bass
Social and Behavioral Science Series
and
the Jossey-Bass
Education Series

Psychoeducational Intervention:
Guidebooks for School Practitioners

Consulting Editors

Charles A. Maher
Rutgers University

Joseph E. Zins
University of Cincinnati

Contents

Part Three: Supporting Community Prevention Programs

Preface

All across our country, adults concerned about the health and development of young people are searching for answers to the problems of alcohol and drug abuse. Although the problems have been with us for a long time, there is a renewed sense of urgency now, when we need more than ever to cultivate the best potential of young Americans.

> A suburban school board meets late into the night, trying to reach agreement on a policy to address the serious high school alcohol problem: weekend drinking parties, beer smuggled into school in book bags, widespread indifference to studies even among some of the most talented students.

> An elementary school principal in a disadvantaged inner-city neighborhood notices more and more fifth graders parroting the street behavior of older

children: hanging out by the corner store known for drug deals, wearing gang colors, carrying drug paraphernalia in their pockets.

In a comfortable small town, the parents of a sixteen-year-old high school junior are stunned when he attempts suicide. Their shock is doubled when the hospital emergency room tells them his blood alcohol is near a lethal level. Later they learn he has been drinking daily after school for months, then falling asleep until they arrive home from work.

We all recognize these stories; they are the reality of our lives. But what are we to do? Until recently we have responded with treatment, which attempts to change problem behaviors after they have surfaced. Unfortunately, our efforts to control drug and alcohol abuse with treatment have been disappointing in several ways. First, treatment for addicted adolescents has shown only modest success. Second, treatment is costly because it must be directed individually at each person with a drug or alcohol problem. Third, the large investment in treatment does nothing to inhibit the spread of the problem to other young people. It is as if we were providing expensive ambulances at the bottom of a cliff to pick up the youngsters who fall off, rather than building a fence at the top to keep them from falling in the first place.

This book is about building that fence. It was written for people who are concerned about the abuse of alcohol and other drugs in their communities and who are committed to stepping in ahead of the problem with solutions that are far reaching and lasting.

Historically, when Americans have been challenged by serious threats such as disease epidemics, they have responded with an all-out effort that includes intensive research, training, and even life-style changes. This book proposes a similar all-out community effort to prevent alcohol and other drug problems through a comprehensive approach, "Communities That Care." The strategy has grown out of a decade of research we have conducted with a team of researchers from the University of Washington and colleagues across the country, building on and integrating diverse research efforts. Our research addresses two lines of inquiry, and it is these two questions that drive the "Communities That Care" strategy:

1. Why are some young people having such serious problems with alcohol and other drugs?
2. What can be done to reduce the risk factors and promote protective factors?

Research has shown that there are a number of *risk factors,* arising throughout the course of child development, that increase the chances of drug and alcohol abuse. Understanding these risk factors is the first step toward identifying effective means of prevention. Equally important is the evidence that certain *protective factors* can help shield youngsters from drug and alcohol problems. If we can reduce risk while increasing protection throughout the course of young people's development, we can prevent these problems and promote healthy, prosocial growth. In our work, we have identified this approach to prevention as the social development strategy.

As our understanding of risk and protective factors has grown, we have searched for effective ways to address them. The "Communities That Care" approach organizes what we have learned about prevention strategies. It incorporates program elements that effectively reduce risk by promoting protective factors.

Because risk is not simple, a comprehensive approach to preventing drug and alcohol problems is needed. This requires broad vision and many participants. The "Communities That Care" strategy described in this book is based not only on identified risk and protective factors and prevention research, but also on years of experience working with dozens of communities to mobilize their citizens and resources to prevent drug abuse.

In developing the "Communities That Care" strategy, we went through a number of steps:

1. We assessed existing theory, research, and practice, exploring factors that place children and youth at risk of developing

drug and alcohol problems (risk factors) and factors that
offer a protective shield (protective factors).

2. We analyzed prevention and early intervention strategies
   to determine which approaches work best and integrated
   them into program elements that address risk factors in families, peer groups, schools, and communities.

3. We developed and field-tested a strategy for mobilizing
   communities to plan and implement their own unique communitywide alcohol and drug abuse prevention efforts. This
   strategy includes involving key community leaders, who set
   up a broad-based community board; the board in turn as-
   sesses the community's current environment for alcohol and
   drug risk, creates an action plan to reduce those risks, and
   secures the support of community members to put the plan
   in motion.

4. We identified training materials and technical assistance
   resources to help communities put programs in place that
   are suited to unique local needs yet are true to the principles identified by research.

5. Finally, we identified structured ways for communities to
   make sure each step of the strategy is carried out well and
   to evaluate the effects of their mobilization efforts on reducing alcohol and other drug abuse.

A community prevention strategy based on risk reduction requires the following:

- A shared definition of the problem
- A unified vision of change
- A developmentally complete series of prevention programs
- A high level of coordination and cooperation among service-
  providing professionals and concerned community members
- Skillful mobilization of human and financial resources

This book offers a framework for developing such a consensus
on the prevention of drug and alcohol problems and for creating a coherent, accountable, and effective community action plan
based on that consensus. It is grounded in theory, research, and

practical experience in risk reduction and community mobilization.

Audience

Communities That Care was written for every person concerned about the healthy, drug-free development of America's children. The prevention of drug abuse requires active involvement by whole communities, from elected leaders to citizens at the grassroots level. This book describes how community members can join together for effective preventive action. It should be useful to mayors and city managers; school boards, school administrators, teachers, counselors, and early childhood educators; police chiefs, sheriffs, crime prevention officers, and DARE officers; medical and health professionals; business people and labor leaders; neighborhood coalition members and communities of faith; social service providers and media representatives; and civic groups and volunteer organizations. Its greatest use will be to help the diverse segments of any community to join together in the common mission of making their community a protective environment for the healthy development of its young people.

Overview of the Contents

The book is organized as a comprehensive guide. Part One, "Preventing Drug Abuse Among Youth at Risk," begins, in Chapter One, with an introduction to the problem. Chapter Two provides the theoretical and empirical underpinnings for the "Communities That Care" strategy. Risk factors for adolescent drug and alcohol abuse are described, protective factors are explained in the context of the social development strategy, and a definition and overview of community mobilization are presented. Chapter Three outlines the "Communities That Care" community mobilization process step by step; it covers who should be involved in the initial phases and how to develop a plan, conduct risk and resource assessments, empower local community ownership of the project, and monitor and evaluate progress.

Part Two is on "Community Action Strategies." Chapter Four, by J. David Hawkins, Janet Y. Miller, and Richard F. Catalano, Jr., offers introductory descriptions of the program element presentations that are given in Chapters Five through Twelve. Chapter Five, by Kathryn E. Barnard, begins at the beginning by looking at risk reduction strategies in the earliest period of development — prenatal and during infancy. The emphasis in this chapter is on the importance of early bonding to family as a lifelong protective factor. Chapter Six focuses on involving the parents of young children as well as preschools or child-care centers in preventing later drug and alcohol problems for high-risk children through early childhood education. It outlines the critical components and criteria for preschool programs that will address risk by building up protective factors early on. Chapter Seven continues along the developmental continuum by describing parent training strategies that address risk and protective factors for parents of children from preschool through early adolescence. Family-related risk and protective factors are targeted by the three parent-training approaches described.

Chapter Eight describes two of the most effective approaches for making schools protective environments for child development: the School Development Program and the Program Development Evaluation method. Effective school management addresses not only risk and protective factors directly related to school performance, but also other critical social and personal factors known to predict later drug and alcohol abuse.

Chapter Nine identifies three distinct but complementary instructional strategies that have been found to increase student commitment to school and to reduce academic failure: proactive classroom management, effective teaching strategies, and cooperative learning. Chapter Ten, by the W. T. Grant Consortium on the School-Based Promotion of Social Competence, offers an overview and set of criteria for evaluating school-based drug and alcohol curricula for their effectiveness in reducing risk and increasing protective factors. Programs that teach clearly identifiable social competencies are described in terms of criteria developed by the consortium.

Chapter Eleven addresses the important arena of school and community drug use policy, and outlines strategies for developing and implementing policy changes at all levels to reduce the risk of alcohol and other drug abuse by young people. Chapter Twelve takes risk reduction to the broadest public arena by outlining a strategy for enlisting all elements of the media in proactive and long-term campaigns to prevent drug and alcohol abuse.

Part Three, "Supporting Community Prevention Programs," tackles the barrier that has stopped many communities from comprehensively addressing the drug and alcohol problem: a shortage of resources. There may be readers who say we cannot afford prevention programs such as those described in this book. Chapter Thirteen, by A. Baron Holmes IV, Gary D. Gottfredson, and Janet Y. Miller, is for the skeptics. The authors offer some perspectives on resources to stimulate new thinking and techniques for securing long-term, stable funding.

Acknowledgments

A book such as this one owes a great debt to countless individuals. As we have said, *Communities That Care* builds on the work of many outstanding theorists, researchers, and program developers from all over the country. We wish to acknowledge with gratitude the contributions of the following colleagues whose work has inspired, informed, and enriched our own. To Denise Gottfredson and Robert J. McMahon for early reviews of the manuscript; to Neil Bracht, Denise Gottfredson, and Gary Gottfredson for major contributions to Chapter Three; to Kathryn Barnard for her authorship of Chapter Five; to Denise Gottfredson for major contributions to Chapter Six; to Kathleen E. Burgoyne, Robert J. McMahon, and Carolyn Webster-Stratton for their review of and input to Chapter Seven; to Suzanne Irvine for her major contribution to the development of Chapter Eight; to James Comer, Norris Haynes, Denise Gottfredson, and Gary Gottfredson for development of Chapter Eight program models; to Carol Cummings for the development of Chapter Nine; to the W. T. Grant Consortium on the School-Based Promotion of Social Competence for Chapter Ten (members of the consortium include Maurice J. Elias, Roger P. Weissberg, Kenneth A. Dodge, J. David Hawkins, Leonard A. Jason, Philip C. Kendall, Cheryl L. Perry, Mary Jane Rotheram-Borus, and Joseph E. Zins); to Ruth Eckland for her contribution to Chapter Eleven and to Lee Dogoloff, Boisson Moore, and James Mosher for their review of and input to the same chapter; to Patricia J. Chappell for her major contribution to Chapter Twelve; and to A. Baron Holmes IV, Gary D. Gottfredson, and Janet Y. Miller for their authorship of Chapter Thirteen. Finally, we are deeply indebted to Hank Resnick, Janet Y. Miller, and Patricia Huling for their editorial assistance in the development of this book.

It is our hope that by providing a framework for preventing the complex and troubling problems of adolescent drug and alcohol abuse, *Communities That Care* will stimulate renewed energy and action on the local level. When equipped with sound information and effective strategies, local community groups have always been effective agents of positive change.

We share the optimism expressed by Margaret Mead in these words: "Never doubt that a small group of committed individuals can change the world. Indeed it is the only thing that ever has." The world of thousands of youngsters at risk of serious alcohol and other drug addiction needs to be changed. Our task here is to provide the information and tools to do the job. With the guidance and commitment of local leaders and citizens, communities can take significant steps toward preventing the personal tragedy and social costs associated with alcohol and other drug abuse among our young people.

Seattle, Washington   J. David Hawkins
June 1992   Richard F. Catalano, Jr.

The Authors

J. David Hawkins is professor of social work and director of the Social Development Research Group of the University of Washington, Seattle. He received his B.A. degree (1967) from Stanford University in sociology and his M.A. (1969) and his Ph.D. (1975) degrees from Northwestern University in sociology.

Hawkins's research focuses on understanding and preventing child and adolescent health and behavior problems. Since 1981, he has been conducting a longitudinal prevention study that is testing a risk reduction strategy based on his theoretical work. He is codeveloper of the social development model, a theory that provides a foundation for delinquency and drug abuse prevention, and he is coauthor of *Preparing for the Drug (Free) Years* (1987, with others) a prevention program that empowers parents to reduce the risks for drug abuse in their families while strengthening family bonding.

Hawkins has served as a member of the Epidemiology, Prevention, and Services Research Review Committee of the

National Institute on Drug Abuse. He is currently a member of the Office for Substance Abuse Prevention's National Advisory Committee on Substance Abuse Prevention and a member of the Committee on Prevention of Mental Disorders of the Institute of Medicine, National Academy of Sciences. He also serves on the National Education Goals Panel Resource Group on Safe and Drug-Free Schools. He is committed to translating research into effective practice and policy to improve adolescent health and development.

Richard F. Catalano, Jr., is associate professor of social work and associate director of the Social Development Research Group of the University of Washington, Seattle. He received his B.A. degree (1973) from the University of Wisconsin in sociology and his M.A. (1976) and Ph.D. (1982) degrees from the University of Washington in sociology.

Catalano's main research and program development activities have been in the areas of drug abuse and delinquency. His work has focused on discovering risk and protective factors and on designing and evaluating programs to address these factors. He is principal investigator or coinvestigator on a number of federal grants in this area of research.

Catalano serves on the National Institute on Drug Abuse's Epidemiology and Prevention Review Committee and on the Washington State Advisory Committee for Alcohol and Substance Abuse. He is the codeveloper of the social development strategy and coauthor of *Preparing for the Drug (Free) Years* (1987, with others).

Kathryn E. Barnard is professor of nursing and adjunct professor of psychology at the University of Washington, Seattle. She received her B.S. degree (1960) from the University of Nebraska in nursing, her M.S.N. degree (1962) from Boston University, and her Ph.D. degree (1972) from the University of Washington in nursing. She is particularly noted for her work on parent-infant interaction and parenting in high-risk families. Many of her research findings have been translated into nursing practice.

Gary D. Gottfredson is principal research scientist at the Center for Social Organization of Schools at Johns Hopkins University. He is a psychologist whose work applies the methods of organization development and evaluation research to improving the effectiveness of schools and other organizations in solving social problems. His research activities are in the areas of the prevention of adolescent problem behavior, personality and career development, and the measurement of human and organizational characteristics.

A. Baron Holmes IV is state budget director for the State of South Carolina, where he directs budget-related planning and program evaluation. He received his B.A. degree (1968) from the Woodrow Wilson School of Public and International Affairs at Princeton University in history and his Ph.D. degree (1972) from the University of Chicago in history. Currently he works on children's policy, heading the South Carolina "Kids Count" Project, which is funded by the Annie E. Casey Foundation, and the South Carolina Middle Grades Policy Initiative, which is funded by the Carnegie Corporation.

Janet Y. Miller is a research and evaluation consultant for prevention and family support programs. She received her B.A. degree (1966) from Seattle Pacific University in English, and her M.S.W. degree (1977) and Ph.D. degree (1989) in social welfare from the University of Washington. Her work in clinical services, program development and research, and child welfare policy has focused on the prevention of child abuse and neglect, prevention of childhood disorders, parent education, and family support.

The William T. Grant Foundation Consortium on the School-Based Promotion of Social Competence seeks to facilitate the implementation, evaluation, and refinement of comprehensive social competence promotion efforts beginning in preschool and continuing through high school. The consortium also seeks to increase awareness regarding the need for and the effects of systematic efforts to promote the social competence of American children and adolescents. The members of the consortium are Maurice J. Elias (Rutgers University) and Roger P. Weissberg (Yale University), co-chairs; J. David Hawkins (University of Washington); Kenneth A. Dodge (Vanderbilt University); Leonard A. Jason (DePaul University); Philip C. Kendall (Temple University); Cheryl L. Perry (University of Minnesota); Mary Jane Rotheram-Borus (Columbia University); and Joseph E. Zins (University of Cincinnati).

COMMUNITIES
THAT CARE

Part One

PREVENTING DRUG ABUSE AMONG YOUTH AT RISK

Chapter 1

The Problem of Alcohol and Other Drug Abuse

The abuse of alcohol and other drugs is a major problem deeply rooted in our society. According to estimates from the Alcohol, Drug Abuse, and Mental Health Administration (Rice, Kelman, Miller, & Dunmeyer, 1990, p. 2) the combined costs of alcohol and other drug abuse in the United States exceeded $144 billion in 1988. But these costs—in lost productivity, health care, law enforcement, and drug treatment—are only the economic costs of drug and alcohol abuse. Behind the monetary costs are ruined lives and devastated families.

All of us feel the effects, even if we are not directly involved. The abuse of alcohol and other drugs has changed our communities and our way of life. Through our children, it is having an impact on our future. Children and youth are more vulnerable to problems associated with alcohol and drug abuse than any other group in society, and whole generations of young people have been affected.

When we talk about drug and alcohol abuse, it is important that we make clear our definition of *abuse*. In this book,

3

adolescent drug abuse will be defined as either the *frequent* use of alcohol or other drugs during the teenage years or the use of alcohol or other drugs *in a manner that leads to problems.* This conception of drug abuse is not meant to condone the infrequent use of alcohol by teenagers, which is a violation of the law and which in itself may lead to problems. It simply recognizes that, in recent decades, a relatively large number of teenagers have tried alcohol or other drugs without becoming frequent users or developing problems related to their use (Shedler & Block, 1990). However, because starting to use alcohol or other drugs early on in a child's development has been shown to increase risk for later drug abuse, early *first* use of alcohol and other drugs by children and adolescents is a major focus of the prevention strategies discussed in this book.

Many strategies for preventing alcohol and other drug problems have been tried over the years. "Communities That Care" proposes that whole communities can become healthier, more productive places for young people and adults alike if people at every level get involved and stay involved long enough to make a difference. Alcohol and other drug problems will diminish through this challenging and rewarding community experience.

What Has Been Tried?

Why is it that many efforts to control alcohol and other drug abuse have met with frustration? We will examine several approaches that have been tried to see why, by themselves, they have failed to control drug abuse.

Controlling the supply of illegal drugs through laws and law enforcement is a constantly growing effort in this country. Tougher drug laws have been passed in recent years, huge seizures of illegal drugs have been made, and increasing numbers of drug dealers have been convicted and jailed. These measures are important and necessary; without them, the drug problem would be worse than it is. But these efforts have not eliminated drug abuse.

Stronger law enforcement does not solve the drug problem because it cannot control the demand for drugs, and, in a large market with high demand, cannot even bring about a degree of scarcity that would make illegal drugs prohibitively expensive. In such a market, suppliers and dealers become so numerous that prices remain relatively low. From 1986 to 1989, federal spending on drug enforcement more than doubled. At the same time, the street price for cocaine dropped from $100 to $75 a gram, according to U.S. Drug Enforcement Agency estimates.

In 1984, a major study of the U.S. drug problem (Polich, Ellickson, Reuter, & Kahan, 1984) concluded that the supply of drugs cannot be eliminated so long as demand is strong. The authors noted that when the demand for drugs is great, neither the supply nor the cost of drugs is much affected when suppliers are shut down, since others soon fill the vacuum thus created. Even doubling enforcement, they say, would have little effect on retail prices.

Efforts from 1919 to 1933 to restrict the supply of alcohol through Prohibition proved unworkable. Today, although alcohol is legally available for adults, we continue to restrict its sale to minors. Even in this we fail: adolescents in virtually every community of our country have little difficulty finding access to alcohol. As with other drugs, as long as the demand for alcohol remains high, youngsters will find ways to obtain it.

Can we reduce demand? Increasingly, law enforcement authorities and policy makers recognize that the solution depends on this. In fact, we have seen declines in the use of illegal drugs in recent years. The National Institute on Drug Abuse's National Household Surveys found that the proportion of the population using illegal drugs in America dropped by 37 percent between 1985 and 1988 and dropped another 11 percent between 1988 and 1990. The proportion of the population using cocaine declined by almost half from 1985 to 1988 and dropped another 29 percent between 1988 and 1990. But these declines are primarily among people who use drugs infrequently. These are people who have a stake in society and in their own future well-being, and they have begun to refrain from drug use because of the risks they see associated with use. During the same period, usage rates *increased* among people who use drugs more frequently — compulsive users and addicts, who have less investment in the future and who appear to be less influenced by the risk of greater enforcement (Office of National Drug Control Policy, 1990). Among adolescents, alcohol has continued to be the pervasive "drug of choice," with usage declining much more slowly than the use of other illegal drugs. In 1990, 57 percent of American high school seniors were currently alcohol drinkers, and 32 percent reported heavy drinking (five or more drinks in a row) in the past two weeks (Johnston, O'Malley, & Bachman, 1991).

Treatment is a strategy to reduce demand among those with the most serious drug and alcohol problems. However, because of the many social and health problems associated with drug use, these individuals have already run up significant costs to society by the time they are treated. And although research on treatment programs has shown that virtually all addicts and alcoholics who wish to stop using can succeed in doing so, a significant number of them do not remain drug-free. About two-thirds of them return to drug use (although not necessarily addiction) within less than a year of treatment (U.S. Surgeon General, 1988). Treatment is necessary and important, but it comes at a point where considerable damage has already been done to the user, people around the user, and society.

Effective Prevention

How can we reduce the demand for alcohol and other drugs *before* problems develop and the costs to individuals, families, and society are incurred? Over the past twenty years, the most widely used method has been school-based drug education. By teaching young people about the dangers of drugs, these programs have sought to dissuade them from starting drug and alcohol use at a most vulnerable stage of development — as they enter the teenage years. Researchers have now learned some important points about the impact of school-based drug education programs:

- By itself, information about the dangers of drugs and alcohol — whether this information is provided through school assemblies or drug education and health courses — has little or no effect on use.
- Short-term approaches — one-shot presentations on alcohol and drugs — are ineffective. Students need to be provided with consistent, extended drug education programs.
- Programs that do affect young people's drug use are those that teach them skills for resisting influences to use alcohol and other drugs and that help them develop strong norms against use. The effects of even these programs, however, often dissipate after two or three years.
- School-based programs that have shown more lasting effects on drug and alcohol use have either offered booster sessions or have broadened the program to involve parents, the communications media, and the community in promoting norms against drug abuse (Pentz, Dwyer, et al., 1989).
- Some school-based programs have proven to be less effective in reducing smoking among children at greatest risk of serious drug abuse than in preventing drug use in the general population (Ellickson & Bell, 1990).

"Communities That Care" has taken this knowledge about the limitations and successes of earlier efforts and used it as a starting point for a new, comprehensive approach.

Chapter 2

Reducing Risk
and Promoting
Positive Social Development

"Communities That Care" is based on a simple premise: in order
to prevent a problem, we must find out what factors increase
the chance of that problem's occurrence and then find ways to
reduce these "risk factors."

There is evidence that a risk reduction approach to prevention is effective. Comprehensive communitywide programs to
reduce risks for heart and lung disease have succeeded in per-
suading people to change their behavior in such areas as diet,
exercise, and smoking (Elder, Molgaard, & Gresham, 1988;
Jacobs et al., 1986; Murray, Davis-Hearn, Goldman, Pirie, &
Luepker, 1988; Vartiainen, Pallonen, McAlister, & Puska,
1990). The studies indicate that prevention strategies undertaken by communities hold great potential for success when they
focus on reducing identified risks in several areas of life.

Over the past thirty years, researchers have identified risk
factors for drug abuse, juvenile delinquency, and related problems. These factors are located in the principal social settings
of our lives — the family, the school, the peer group, the community — and within individuals themselves. The more risk fac-

tors present in a community, the greater the likelihood of drug and alcohol abuse in that community. The more risk factors to which an individual is exposed, the greater the likelihood that the individual will become involved in drug and alcohol abuse. If we can reduce or counter these risk factors in young people's lives, we have a good chance of preventing drug abuse.

Risk factors for adolescent drug and alcohol abuse have been identified in two general areas: (1) in the broad social context or environment in which people develop, such as the community and the neighborhood, and (2) within the individual and the individual's relationship with the family, the school, and peers. Elsewhere, we have published a comprehensive review of these risk factors (Hawkins, Catalano, & Miller, 1992). We summarize them in Exhibit 2.1. Readers interested in the research studies that identified these risk factors are referred to Hawkins, Catalano, and Miller (1992) as well as to Kandel, Simcha-Fagan, and Davis (1986), Newcomb, Maddahian, and Bentler (1986), and Simcha-Fagan, Gersten, and Langner (1986).

Economic and social deprivation is the first environmental risk factor for drug abuse. Children who live in deteriorating and crime-ridden neighborhoods where there is little hope for a better

Exhibit 2.1. Risk Factors for Adolescent Drug Abuse.

Environmental Risk Factors
- Economic and social deprivation
- Low neighborhood attachment and community disorganization
- Transitions and mobility
- Community laws and norms favorable toward drug use
- Availability

Individual Risk Factors
- Family history of alcoholism
- Poor family management practices
- Early antisocial behavior with aggressiveness
- Parental drug use and positive attitudes toward use
- Academic failure
- Low commitment to school
- Alienation or rebelliousness
- Antisocial behavior in early adolescence
- Association with drug-using peers
- Favorable attitudes toward drugs
- Early first use of drugs

---

future are more likely to engage in delinquent behavior. Children who come from economically deprived areas and who also have behavior and other adjustment problems early in life are more likely to have problems with drugs later on.

A related but separate risk factor is *low neighborhood attachment and community disorganization*. Communities or neighborhoods where people have little attachment to the community, where there are few strong social institutions, and where there is low surveillance of public places have higher rates of adult and juvenile crime and drug trafficking.

Transitions and mobility—even normal school transitions—are statistically related to increases in problem behaviors. When children move from elementary school to middle or junior high school, significant increases in the rate of drug use and other problem behavior often occur. Communities that are characterized by high rates of movement between schools or residences appear to have a greater risk of drug problems. Although some people can buffer the negative effects of moving by quickly making connections with people in new communities, others lack the resources or skills to do so.

Community laws and norms, the attitudes and policies a community holds, form an important risk factor if they favor drug use. Norms are communicated in obvious and subtle ways: through laws and written policies, through informal social practices, and through the expectations of parents and other members of the community. One example of a law affecting drug use is the taxation of alcoholic beverages: higher rates of taxation have been shown to decrease the rate of alcohol use at every level of use. Other examples of local rules and norms are policies and regulations in schools and workplaces, which are also linked with rates of drug and alcohol use in those settings. When laws, tax rates, and community standards are favorable toward alcohol and other drug use, or even when they are just unclear, young people are at higher risk for drug abuse.

The *availability* of drugs in the broad social environment also contributes to risk. The more available drugs and alcohol are in a community, the higher the risk that the community's young people will abuse drugs. A higher rate of drug use has been found in schools where children perceive that drugs are more available, even after controlling for other factors.

Other risk factors for drug abuse have been identified in characteristics of the individual child and of the child's primary relationships—the family, the school, and the peer group. Many of these factors also predict juvenile delinquency. These individual risk factors are presented here in the order in which they appear or become influential as the child matures.

When children are born or raised in a family with *a history of alcoholism,* their risk of having alcohol or other drug problems themselves increases. Being raised in a family with an alcoholic member increases risk for both boys and girls, although a genetic link has been established only for boys. The risk of alcoholism appears to increase two- to fourfold for a boy born of alcoholic parents.

Poor family management practices have been shown to increase the risk of drug abuse, whether or not there are family drug problems. A lack of clear expectations for behavior, failure of parents to keep track of their children (knowing where they are and with whom), and excessively severe or inconsistent punishment are among the family management practices that may lead to problems.

Early aggressiveness has been identified as a risk factor among boys. Boys who are aggressive in kindergarten through third grade have been found to be at higher risk for later substance abuse. When a boy's aggressive behavior in the early grades is combined with either extreme shyness or hyperactivity, there is an even greater risk of problems in adolescence.

Children whose parents use illegal drugs, are heavy users of alcohol, or are tolerant of children's use are more likely to become drug abusers in adolescence. This risk posed by *parental drug use and positive attitudes toward use* increases further if parents involve children in their own drug or alcohol use—for example, asking the child to light the parent's cigarette or get the parent a beer from the refrigerator.

Beginning in the late elementary grades, *academic failure* increases the risk of both drug abuse and delinquency. Although children fail for many reasons, it appears that the experience of failure itself increases the risk of problem behaviors. *Low commitment to school* is a risk factor that is often associated with academic failure. The child has ceased to see the role of student as viable.

Children who experience *alienation or rebelliousness* are at higher risk of drug abuse. Such youngsters may feel they are not part of society and thus not bound by its rules; they may not believe in trying to be successful or responsible and may take an actively antagonistic stance toward society. *Antisocial behavior in early adolescence* is a risk factor that includes misbehaving in school, skipping school, getting into fights with other children, and being involved in delinquent behavior. Children who engage in these behaviors are also at increased risk for drug abuse.

Children who *associate with peers who are using drugs* are much more likely to use drugs themselves. This is one of the most consistent predictors identified by research. Even when children come from well-managed families and do not experience other risk factors, simply associating with friends who use drugs greatly increases their risk.

Favorable attitudes toward drugs often begin in middle school, as children begin to know others who are trying drugs. In elementary school, children usually express antidrug attitudes and have difficulty imagining why people use drugs. With greater acceptance comes increased risk that a child will also use drugs.

Early first use of drugs greatly increases the likelihood that children will have problems with alcohol or other drugs later on. The earlier young people try alcohol or other drugs, the greater the risk. Research shows that young people who initiate alcohol or other drug use before the age of fifteen are at twice the risk of having drug problems when compared with those who wait until after the age of nineteen (Robins & Przybeck, 1985).

Although at least sixteen risk factors for drug abuse have been identified, most of the recent studies of alcohol and drug abuse prevention have focused on only two risk factors: (1) favorable attitudes toward drug and alcohol use and (2) social influences to use drugs and alcohol.

Experimental efforts to change attitudes and enhance skills to resist drug influences — usually in the form of school programs targeting middle school children — have shown short-term success in preventing and reducing smoking (see Botvin, 1986; Bukoski, 1986; Flay, 1985; Moskowitz, 1989; Murray et al., 1988; Murray, Pirie, Luepker, & Pallonen, 1989; Murray, Richards, Luepker, & Johnson, 1987; Schinke, Bebel, Orlandi, & Botvin, 1988; Schinke, Botvin, et al., 1988; Tobler, 1986; Vartiainen, Pallonen, McAlister, Koskela, & Puska, 1983, 1986; Vartiainen et al., 1990), and less consistently, in preventing and reducing alcohol and marijuana use (Botvin, 1986; Ellickson & Bell, 1990; Hansen, Johnson, Flay, Graham, & Sobel, 1988; McAlister, Perry, Killen, Slinkard, & Maccoby, 1980; Pentz, Dwyer, et al., 1989). The most durable positive effects have come from interventions addressing these risk factors in several domains: school, family, and the larger community (Johnson et al., 1989; Pentz, Dwyer, et al., 1989). They have also come from the use of booster sessions to keep the students' normative commitments strong over time (Ellickson & Bell, 1990). However, even booster sessions did not sustain initial positive effects on alcohol use beyond the seventh-grade intervention year in the Ellickson and Bell study. The researchers hypothesize that the erosion of effects occurred because of the wide acceptance of alcohol use throughout society. Sustained reductions in teenage drinking may require multifaceted interventions supporting community-level change.

Ellickson and Bell (1990) also found that a curriculum emphasizing clear nonuse norms and social influence resistance skills actually produced higher smoking rates among children who already were smoking by seventh grade. These were children characterized by risk factors that appear earlier in childhood, including poor family communication, academic failure, low commitment to school, and early behavior problems. These results have underscored the need for risk reduction interventions that affect more of the identified risk factors for drug abuse and that address these risk factors earlier in children's development. There is evidence that risk increases exponentially with the number of risk factors experienced over the course of development (Newcomb et al., 1986). We know that several factors become stable predictors of risk during the elementary grades. Preventive interventions that reduce multiple risk factors prior to drug initiation may hold the greatest promise for drug abuse prevention.

The Social Development Strategy: Protecting Against Risk

Many young people do not abuse drugs even though they have been exposed to risk factors. Working in these youngsters' favor, balancing the risk factors in their lives, are "protective factors": qualities or conditions that moderate the effects of exposure to risk. The "Communities That Care" strategy is designed to enhance protective factors while reducing risks, to promote wholesome behavior leading to health, well-being, and personal success.

The emphasis on building up protection while reducing risk distinguishes the "Communities That Care" approach to risk reduction. The program's theoretical framework, called the social development model, incorporates an understanding of both the factors leading to problems in adolescence (risk factors) and the factors leading to healthy development (protective factors). The model has theoretical roots in control theory (Hirschi, 1969) and social learning theory (Akers, 1977; Bandura, 1977), but it goes beyond these theories. The social development model emphasizes the importance of bonding as a key protective factor. It specifies how bonding develops.

Research has demonstrated that healthy bonding is a significant factor in children's resistance to crime and drugs. Strong positive bonds have three important components: (1) *attachment* — positive relationships with others; (2) *commitment* — an investment in the future; and (3) *belief* about what is right and wrong, with an orientation to positive, moral behavior and action. Antidrug attitudes are strengthened by promoting adolescents' bonds, including relationships with non-drug users, commitment to the various social groups in which they are involved (families, schools, community, prosocial peer groups), and values and beliefs regarding what is healthy and ethical behavior.

How does bonding develop? The social development model identifies three conditions that create social bonding: opportunity, skills, and recognition. First, the *opportunity* to be an active contributor or member of a group could mean feeding the gerbils or cleaning the chalkboard in first grade, or helping plan family outings or cook family meals as a young adolescent. Making a meaningful contribution to the family, school, or community is critical to becoming bonded to that unit. Second, having the *skills* to be successful in contributing to the social unit promotes bonding. Giving children new responsibilities at home or school provides them with opportunities, but unless they have the skills to carry out those responsibilities, the opportunities may become burdens of frustration and failure. Children need a wide variety of skills to be successful. Third, a system of consistent *recognition* or reinforcement is essential. Children, like adults, need to know when they are doing well. Praise or recognition reinforces children's efforts and makes them feel accepted and bonded.

Research has demonstrated that young people who are strongly bonded to parents, to school, to non-drug-using peers, and to their communities are less likely to engage in behaviors disapproved by these groups because such behaviors threaten those bonds. The social development strategy enhances positive bonds while reducing risk factors, so that children are doubly protected.

When people feel bonded to society, or to a social unit like the family or school, they want to live according to its standards or norms: "If you feel you belong in the system, you play by its rules; if you play by the rules, you are more likely to succeed; if you succeed you are accepted by, and hence feel you belong in, the system" (Berrueta-Clement et al., 1984, p. 74). Clear standards are very important, so as not to confuse children. This is particularly true of standards about alcohol and other drug use. Today's families, schools, and communities need clearly stated guidelines on alcohol and other drug use, letting children know what is and is not acceptable for people their age.

Whatever the setting, there are several keys to establishing and upholding new standards or norms regarding the use of alcohol and other drugs.

- Set clear guidelines for behavior.
- Monitor children's behavior to determine if they are following the guidelines.
- Recognize and reinforce children for following the guidelines and see that there are consistent and moderate negative consequences for violating the guidelines.
- Teach skills for resisting negative influences. To be bonded, children need the skills necessary for meaningful involvement in their families, schools, and communities; to resist negative influences, they also need the skills to abide by anti-drug norms. They may want to follow the guidelines against drug use, but unless they know how to resist peer influences, they may be unsuccessful.

Without positive bonds to the family, school, and community, and without clear guidelines against drug use, young people are more likely to abuse alcohol and other drugs. This is particularly true when children have friends who use drugs. However, a youngster who is bonded to people and institutions that have clear norms against drug use is less likely to get involved with drug-using peers, for such association could threaten valued bonds. Figure 2.1 is a picture of the social development strategy, showing how these concepts are related.

We saw earlier that some forms of drug use have declined in recent years, most notably the casual use of various illegal drugs. Many people are saying, "It's no longer worth the risk to use drugs." An important characteristic of these people, which distinguishes them from those who start using tobacco, alcohol, or other drugs early, is that they are bonded: they have a stake in society and feel connected to it. They have a good reason not to use drugs.

One of the strengths of the social development strategy as the basis for designing drug and alcohol abuse prevention programs is that the framework of risk and protective factors can be applied to many adolescent problems other than substance abuse. Other teenage health and behavior problems are currently the focus of heightened concern, including school dropout, teen pregnancy, and crime (Schorr, 1988). Many of

Figure 2.1. The Social Development Strategy.

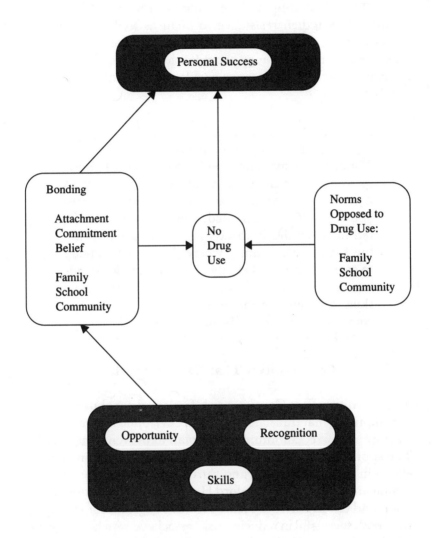

the risk factors identified for drug and alcohol abuse are also predictive of these problems (Dryfoos, 1990), and the protective factors of bonding and clear behavioral norms have been shown to strengthen resistance to them as well. The focus of this book is on preventing alcohol and drug problems, but the social development strategy promotes healthy, prosocial development in ways that counteract a wide range of adolescent problem behaviors.

Bonding in Your Own Life
Think of an experience you have had being bonded to someone, a time when you were very close to a person who was in a position to guide you or help you — someone you trusted, valued, were committed to. How did it affect your behavior? Is yours the kind of community where people are bonded to each other and where the opportunities for bonding are plentiful? If not, creating opportunities, skills, and reinforcements for young people in your community is especially important.

"Communities That Care" Overview

"Communities That Care" is a risk-focused drug abuse prevention approach that translates the social development strategy into a comprehensive, communitywide plan to prevent drug abuse. The approach draws from previous communitywide prevention efforts in the United States and Europe that have demonstrated significant impact. The Stanford Heart Disease Prevention Program and the Minnesota Heart Health Program, for example, were both successful in reducing risks associated with heart disease (Carlaw, Mittelmark, Bracht, & Luepker, 1984; Flora, Maccoby, & Farquhar, 1989). These projects employed mass media, community mobilization, voluntarism, and educational strategies (Farquhar, 1985; Farquhar et al., 1984; Perry, Klepp, & Sillers, 1989). The Midwestern Primary Prevention Project used similar strategies in Kansas City to achieve significant reductions in adolescent drug use (Pentz, Dwyer, et al., 1989).

There are several advantages to a communitywide approach. Risk and protective factors are lodged in all aspects of the community; in schools, families, individuals, and the community itself. Community efforts can affect the entire local environment, including community norms, values, and policies (Bracht, 1990). Involving the whole community facilitates widespread communication to achieve consistent norms about drug use and the need for prevention, as well as knowledge about risk and protective factors. A communitywide approach can also promote the development of strong bonds to family, school, and the community itself among young people.

Because community approaches are likely to involve a wide spectrum of individuals, groups, and organizations, they create a broad base of support for behavior change. Unhealthful behaviors like alcohol and other drug abuse are increasingly viewed as unacceptable in communities with broad involvement in prevention. Costs, too, are reduced by broad-based involvement of volunteers (and one by-product is likely to be lowered costs for professional intervention and treatment).

The firm support of community leaders and their involvement in a prevention effort are likely to lead to long-term change. The reallocation of resources to reduce risk becomes feasible with support from key community leaders. Programs and strategies gradually become integrated into the regular services and activities of local organizations and institutions. The communitywide focus creates a synergy: the whole is more powerful than all of its parts would be, working separately.

The community mobilization strategy of "Communities That Care" described in this book is not meant to be a rigid approach. Many communities are already engaged in efforts to reduce drug and alcohol abuse among their young people. Neither the community mobilization strategy nor the specific program elements described in this book are meant to be "cookie cutters" to stamp out identical projects. Each community can use the principles and prevention models outlined here to create a communitywide risk reduction strategy that satisfies local needs.

The "Communities That Care" strategy is designed to proceed through two phases: Phase I, community mobilization, analysis of risks and resources, and action planning; and Phase II, implementation of prevention strategies and programs to reduce risk factors.

Phase I introduces the community to a process that leads to communitywide mobilization to carry out the community board's action plan. This phase is designed to bring together representatives of community groups, agencies, organizations, and service providers under the umbrella of the community board. Ultimately, the board takes the lead in drug abuse prevention efforts throughout the community, creating a common vision of prevention and a unified strategy for action by the whole community. The first activity in Phase I is the decision by key leaders in the community to participate in the planning process and form a community board to oversee the program. Once the board has been formed and trained, its Phase I tasks are to conduct a community risk and resource assessment and create an action plan for communitywide drug abuse prevention.

Phase I: Initiating the Process

1. Orientation of key leaders and formation of community board (may include key leaders or their designates)
2. Community board training
3. Community risk assessment and creation of prevention action plan by community board

"Communities That Care" helps community boards develop action plans that meet local needs and priorities. At the conclusion of Phase I, community boards have a clear picture of the community's risk profile and priority risk factors. They also review both local programs and the program interventions described in this book, incorporating elements they find to be appropriate to their own community's risks and resources. Each program element in the "Communities That Care" strategy is grounded in reliable research and evaluation, addresses factors that place children at risk for drug abuse, and is consistent with the social development strategy. In Phase II, community boards implement the program elements they have specified in their action plans.

Phase II: Program Planning and Implementation

1. Formation of program task forces
2. Development of program funding and support systems
3. Monitoring and evaluation of implementation

The "Communities That Care" program elements are divided into three general areas of focus: preschool/family, school, and community.

Preschool and Family Elements

- Pre- and postnatal strategies for promoting early parent-child bonding.
- Educational programs to benefit children aged two to five through parent training and center-based activities. Parents, child-care workers, and teachers learn ways to promote language and reading skills, provide opportunities for active learning, build positive ways to set and enforce clear rules, and learn how to help children manage their own behavior.
- Parent training to improve family management skills in areas such as communication, problem solving, creating clear family expectations (such as setting limits and establishing effective rewards or punishment), and managing children's problem behaviors in positive ways. The parent training programs are appropriate not only for parents but for all adults responsible for raising children, including foster parents, grandparents, and day-care workers. Each of the three recommended programs targets the management of children at different developmental stages. The first, aimed at the earliest stage, focuses on family management; the second focuses on academic success; and the third prepares families of children entering the high-risk years for drug initiation.

School Elements

- School organization, development, and management for parents, teachers, mental health staff, and administrators at the school level. This program element includes a data-based method for discovering, acting on, and monitoring the effectiveness of changes in school practices and organizational arrangements.
- Instructional improvement training for teachers. Teachers learn ways to improve their instructional practices, including the use of proactive classroom management, interactive teaching, and cooperative learning methods. They also learn peer coaching techniques to support their colleagues in adopting these new skills.
- Evaluation criteria to help communities choose school curricula that teach social competencies. Many such curricula are available, including those that teach young people to resist pro-drug social influences from peers and the media.

Community Elements

- Procedures for assessing, developing, revising, publicizing, and carrying out school and community policies to reduce tobacco, alcohol, and other drug use.
- Media mobilization to educate representatives of the media about the ways children are placed at risk for drug abuse and what protective actions can be taken. Task force members appointed by the community board learn how to work with local media to develop coordinated, long-term campaigns that promote standards opposing the use of alcohol, tobacco, and other drugs by youth. The communications media are an important component of any comprehensive community strategy, since they are in a strong position to provide visibility and create a favorable environment for other program elements.

Financial Resources

- A creative approach to fundraising that connects risk-focused prevention strategies with existing funding sources not normally considered for alcohol and other drug abuse prevention.

These are the program elements of the "Communities That Care" strategy. Community boards will choose those elements most directly targeted to reduce risk factors they have prioritized for action. Boards will often decide to include existing community prevention programs in their risk reduction action plans as well. Community boards should keep clearly in mind the goal of reducing risk factors for drug abuse while enhancing protective factors. It is important to select elements that show promise in accomplishing this goal in your own community. To ensure broad communitywide action across social institutions, at least one program element should be chosen for each of the three arenas: family, school, and community.

Some communities may already have a community mobilization plan in place. For these communities, the "Communities That Care" approach can be useful in determining the promise of existing activities. They can be screened to learn what risk factors they address and how well they are enhancing the protective factors of bonding and clear norms for behavior. Since the "Communities That Care" strategy addresses generic risk factors for adolescent problem behaviors and incorporates a wide range of prevention strategies, communities can use it to focus their mobilization efforts on risk reduction through enhancement of protective factors.

The "Communities That Care" strategy for community mobilization (1) empowers communities to use the recent research on risk and protective factors to guide their mobilization efforts; (2) includes a developmentally complete set of prevention programs targeting families, schools, and communities; (3) includes risk and resource assessment as a tool for focusing and selecting risk reduction activities; (4) is guided by a strategy that ensures that the community's diverse prevention efforts work harmoniously toward a common goal; and (5) makes research-supported prevention models available for community use.

"Communities That Care" has established the following action and knowledge goals for communitywide prevention efforts:

Action Goals

- To use the best available knowledge to develop a comprehensive drug and alcohol abuse prevention strategy, reduce risk factors, increase protective factors, and reduce alcohol and other drug abuse
- To empower communities to plan and implement a comprehensive, communitywide approach to drug and alcohol abuse prevention, using the social development strategy

Knowledge Goal

- To track the effects of the "Communities That Care" activities on risk and protective factors and drug abuse

The "Communities That Care" strategy puts research into action through a comprehensive model that can effectively confront the serious drug and alcohol problems threatening our youth.

Chapter 3

Mobilizing the Community

Research findings suggest a more comprehensive and long-term commitment to drug and alcohol abuse prevention than most communities have engaged in to this point. This chapter describes a community mobilization process for developing a comprehensive, risk-focused, communitywide prevention approach using the social development strategy. Other community mobilization models use elements of the approach described here. However, "Communities That Care" is a process of community mobilization designed to meet the criteria of the social development strategy — that is, to reduce risk by enhancing the protective factors of bonding and clear norms against use. The overview contained in this chapter serves as an introduction and orientation to this process. Full implementation can be facilitated by consultation, training, technical assistance, and resource materials available from the resources at the end of the chapter.

Several kinds of communities may choose to use the "Communities That Care" strategy. For example, a city, a neighborhood within a city, a high school and the schools that feed into it, a small town, a rural county, or a Native American community can use the strategy. The most important requirement is that the community be a clearly defined geographical area and identified as a community by people who live and work there. The smaller and more clearly defined the community, the more effectively it can be mobilized. Larger and more geographically dispersed communities are more difficult to mobilize, but the community must be large enough to have access to the resources to successfully implement their strategy.

The "Communities That Care" community mobilization process consists of two phases: Phase I, a year-long education, risk assessment, and planning phase, and Phase II, actual implementation of the selected program elements (introduced in Chapter Two and described in detail in Part Two of this book).

Phase I (Year 1): Setting the Stage

The first-year activities, emphasizing assessment and planning, in themselves address the risk factors of community disorganization and norms favorable to drug use. These activities involve key leaders and activists from different segments of the community in developing a base of common knowledge leading to an action plan. This process enhances the protective factors of community bonding and clear norms against drug use as the participants work together to assess their community's risk factors. During this first year, community members become actively involved in planning a comprehensive, communitywide approach to prevention based on their own assessment of the risk factors in their community (see Exhibit 3.1).

Community capacity building, board development, local risk and resource assessments, and action planning fill the first year. No other programs are implemented during this time. The premise is that new programs cannot be chosen and implemented effectively until the risk assessment and planning process is complete.

Exhibit 3.1. First-Year Goals and Objectives (Phase I).

Goals

- To reduce community disorganization and change community norms favorable toward drug use
- To create opportunities for involvement of key leaders across program areas, to increase the community members' skills in risk-based prevention planning, to promote recognition for skillful planning efforts, and to enhance bonding of community members across program areas

Objectives

- To involve key leaders in the community from the outset, leading to the establishment of a community board to oversee the program, accountable to the key leaders for progress and results
- To create a community board responsible for conducting a community risk and resource assessment, developing an action plan, and monitoring implementation of the plan
- To develop an action plan compatible with resources, groups, and programs already operating in the community
- To establish the "Communities That Care" effort for a minimum of three years
- To empower communities to take ownership of their action plans so that effective programs will continue beyond the initial stage of enthusiastic support
- To prepare communities to evaluate their own efforts: What parts of the process are effective and what is the total impact of the project?

Step 1: Involve Key Leaders

Key community leaders—at a minimum the mayor, the superintendent of schools, the community's lead law enforcement official, and a business leader—are essential to mobilization. They have the status and authority in their communities to launch an initiative of this magnitude. Their leadership, approval, and support strengthen current policies and provide the resources for carrying out the prevention plan. They are in a position to hold the community board accountable for planning and carrying out the strategy.

This book can be a tool for informing key leaders about the project and letting them know what their role will be, so that they can make a decision about whether to involve their community in "Communities That Care." A major responsibility of the key leaders' group will be to expand ownership of the program in the community by forming a community board with fifteen to twenty members vested with overall authority for operating the program.

Orienting key leaders to the "Communities That Care" approach is an essential first step in the community mobilization strategy. The orientation should provide key leaders with an understanding of the risk-focused approach to prevention and the community mobilization process. It should include presentations on the risk factors for adolescent problem behaviors, the social development strategy, a rationale and steps for forming a community board and holding it accountable, and a review of promising drug abuse prevention approaches. Key leaders are informed about the next steps they will take if they decide to pursue the strategy. Orientation helps key leaders do the following:

- Find a vision of common goals for their community.
- Reach a common understanding of prevention as a comprehensive, long-term, risk-focused effort.
- Decide whether to launch "Communities That Care" in their community.
- Explore who needs to be on the community board to make it function effectively.
- Start a list of people to contact for community board membership.
- Create an accountability mechanism to be used in establishing the community board.

The orientation helps key leaders consider factors that could support a community mobilization effort against drug abuse and those that could stand in its way. The following checklist, adapted from Gottfredson (1988), is a guide in assessing a community's readiness for change:

- Is there cooperation and support among people in community organizations?
- Is there a willingness among community leaders to experi-

ment with change efforts—that is, to test innnovations before making wholesale changes?

- Are problems openly identified?
- Is there a sense of hope in the community, or do leaders feel overwhelmed by the community's problems?
- Can community leaders openly anticipate obstacles and develop strategies to cope with them?
- Is there a willingness to hear both good and bad news?
- Have teams of people worked together in the community to accomplish civic actions in the past?
- Are outside consultants, trainers, or facilitators welcomed in the community?

The process of "forecasting" the community's capacity for change will continue during the next three steps, as more people from the community become involved.

Step 2: Form a Community Board

Once the key leaders have decided to launch the program in their community, the next step is to invite the proposed members of their community board to participate. This board will become the main body for carrying out the day-to-day operations of the program. Some of the key leaders may decide to become members of the board, but all the key leaders together should establish a mechanism to hold the board accountable for progress.

Key leaders will explain what is expected of the board members, how long the process will take, and how (and if) people will be compensated or their expenses for participation covered, if appropriate. Key leaders will make it clear that board members are expected to remain involved for at least three years, meet at least once a month, and present written quarterly reports to the key leaders' group.

Depending on the size of the community, the board will involve fifteen to twenty people, who should represent a variety of community constituencies. The schools, law enforcement, and local social and health service providers should be represented. Other members should represent parent groups, drug treatment programs, youth groups, local businesses, service and civic organizations, religious organizations, recreational organizations, grassroots community coalitions, and the communications media. Every community has people who get things done even though they may not occupy high-level positions. Since board members will plan and oversee implementation of the entire "Communities That Care" project, they need to be people who have a reputation for getting things done in the community. "Communities That Care" requires the involvement of activists from many different sectors of the community.

Communities initiating the "Communities That Care" program should also consider identifying or hiring a project director, whose main responsibility will be to coordinate the activities of the board, guide and monitor the group's progress and achievements, and help the board with community problem solving.

In summary, key leaders and community boards have very different roles to play. Key leaders make a commitment to support the program, select the community board and hold it accountable for progress, and keep the program in the public eye for a period of several years. The members of the community board are likely to be people who are already on the line — either as professionals or as volunteers — in planning, organizing, carrying out, and evaluating the kinds of programs and services the project will offer to children, families, and the larger community. They will assess the community's risks and resources, develop a plan for communitywide risk reduction, and ultimately carry out their action plan.

The first two steps of the mobilization process — involving key leaders and forming a community board — are usually accomplished in three months. Participation as a member of the community board should begin with a series of training events, one for each of the next steps.

Step 3: Conduct a Community Risk Assessment

Community boards should learn how to assess their community's risk factors, as described in Chapter Two. This step builds on key leaders' earlier assessment of the community's readiness for change. Community board members should be trained and prepared to achieve the following:

- Understand the purpose of the project in both its phases and the importance of the community mobilization effort for subsequent risk reduction efforts.
- Understand the risk factors, protective factors, and social development strategy and be able to explain them to others.
- Carry out a community risk assessment.
- Examine existing local programs to determine how well they reduce risk factors and increase protective factors.
- Work together as a team.

Risk assessment is the major focus of this first step of community board action. The risk assessment of "Communities That Care" is tailored to each community, based on local demographics, needs, and resources. The central goal of risk assessment is to draw a portrait of the community that shows the risk status of the whole as well as that of subunits. Many kinds of information—including surveys, observations, public records, and other forms of recorded data—will help assess risks. For example:

- Public records, including data from the census describing single-parent households, poverty, health, and mental health
- Records from police departments and social service agencies regarding neighborhood crime, drug availability, and child abuse
- Records documenting the educational system, including student achievement, dropouts, absenteeism, discipline problems, suspensions, and expulsions
- Survey data to assess the climate and levels of bonding in schools and other community organizations, drug use, and attitudes toward alcohol and other drugs

We have created a risk and resource assessment tool to help community board members assess risk factors in their community and to assess existing community resources that may already address risk and protective factors. This helps the board to be fully prepared to conduct a thorough risk assessment and review all of the community's existing prevention activities.

The board should expect to spend four months in risk assessment, taking a realistic look at the community's exposure to risk factors and how it is addressing and countering them. In assessing risk factors and local program delivery, the board will focus on the extent of risk and the effect local programs are having on identified risk factors—that is, they will assess *outcomes*. Instead of rushing to implement a program, the board uses this process to identify what the levels of risk factors are in the community, to identify specific subcommunities where risk exposure may be particularly high, and then to select the most effective program elements to address the major risks identified.

Step 4: Plan the Program

Once the community board has completed its risk and resource assessment, the next step is strategic planning. Training for this step should teach board members how to draw connections between identified risks and effective programs that address those risks. During step 4, training and planning, the community board begins to develop its action plan. In step 4, the board should do the following:

- Assess the information it has collected about community risk factors and resources.
- Learn to formulate goals and objectives for an action plan to address the risks identified through the community assessment process.
- Establish procedures for choosing program elements to address priority risk factors in the community.
- Conduct an "element fair" consisting of in-depth overviews, including research evidence and supporting materials, of each of the risk reduction program elements under consideration for Phase II.

- Develop a preliminary action plan, including specific program elements to use in the community and a schedule and critical benchmarks for implementation.
- Identify obstacles to carrying out the plan and resources for overcoming those obstacles.
- Develop strategies for redefining jobs and roles of board members representing community agencies and organizations to ensure completion of the action plan on schedule.
- Establish task forces to oversee each program element.
- Select appropriate program evaluation methods.

In creating their action plan, each board will choose three to five high-priority risk factors on which to focus. These risk factors will be matched with the program elements described in Part Two, which are consistent with the social development strategy. Here are some examples of possible choices:

If this risk factor is a problem . . .	. . . then this might be a program or service to implement
Family management	Parent training/education
Aggressiveness of children in the early elementary grades	Early childhood education
Academic failure/little commitment to school (upper elementary grades)	Instructional improvement
High rates of school transition and mobility	School organization, management, and development

To complete the action plan, the community board will need to assign specific roles and responsibilities of the members. Task forces—whose members are drawn from a variety of organizations and agencies to augment the community board—should be formed for each program element in the board's action plan. Each task force is charged with specific aspects of program planning and implementation related to its specific element.

Task force members should be people who represent important constituencies for the specific effort and who have the requisite knowledge, experience, skills, and authority to carry out their task force responsibilities. A task force for media mobilization, for example, might consist of representatives of the community board, city government, concerned citizens, and leaders of print and broadcast media and advertising agencies in the community. Task forces should have formal responsibility for carrying out the work of the board. Besides the task forces established for each program element in the action plan, other task forces may be needed in response to specific local needs. Some boards have, for instance, created a task force focused on board recruitment and training to maintain the vitality of the board over many years.

For lasting change, it is best if the responsibilities of task force members become part of their jobs or roles within their own organizations. For example, if the director or manager of an agency were assigned to a task force, serving as a task force member and carrying out responsibilities on the task force would become part of that person's redefined job. Job redefinition should be anticipated and planned for. Otherwise, people assigned to the task force may feel that there are conflicting demands on their time between the job they have been doing and their new responsibilities to the task force. Some old responsibilities may need to be reassigned to allow time for task force work.

Several different kinds of evaluation will be necessary as the program takes shape in participating communities. Planning for evaluation must begin in the earliest stages. "Communities That Care" has two major evaluation goals, which have to do with process and outcome.

Once the community board and task forces have the information they need to plan an effective program with various elements, *process evaluation* is conducted to help improve program implementation while it is in progress. This contributes to the evaluation of the project as a whole. Process evaluation will seek answers to questions such as these:

- How well is the program working?
- Are we getting the participation we want and need?
- Are the participants learning the skills we are teaching?
- Did we deliver the services we said we would deliver?

More specific questions will need to be answered for each program element. For example, for the parent training element, the evaluation may address questions like these:

- Are parents whose children have been exposed to multiple risk factors participating in training?
- Have participating parents taught their children refusal skills as a result of parent training?

Formulating the right questions is essential to successful evaluation. Training and technical assistance can empower board and task force members to formulate questions that will yield reliable information about how well the overall program and its various component elements are working.

The second major evaluation goal is to determine the impact of the program on the community, called *outcome evaluation*. Outcome evaluation, based on data similar to those gathered for the initial risk assessment, focuses on specific risk factors, drug use, and drug-related problems in the community. The original risk assessment serves as a baseline against which to assess community progress in risk reduction during Phase II. For each program element chosen, specific risk and drug use indicators should be assessed before the program is implemented, at periodic intervals during program delivery, and after the program is completed. Examples of process and outcome measures for each program element are presented in Part Two of this book.

To ensure successful evaluation, the community board should establish an evaluation task force to monitor ongoing evaluation activities. In addition to community board members on this task force, other members might include university researchers, school district evaluators, and other private and public sector representatives with experience in program evaluation.

Phase II: Turning Action Plans into Action

The year-long Phase I effort has now produced a unique community action plan. Figure 3.1 provides the overall timelines for Phases I and II of the "Communities That Care" strategy through year 3. At the beginning of year 2, risk factors and resources have been assessed, program elements have been chosen, and the key leaders, community board, and task forces stand ready to implement them.

Step 5: Establish, Institutionalize, and Evaluate

In this step, the community board moves from planning into specific programmatic action. At this time, community board members focus on implementation of program elements selected during the risk assessment and planning process.

Figure 3.1. Timelines for Initiating Communities That Care.

Timeline for Phase I (Year 1)

Months

```
    1    2    3    4    5    6    7    8    9   10   11   12
    ├ - - ┤
S   1. Involve
T      key leaders
E       │
P           2. Key leader
               orientation
            ├ - - - - ┤
            3. Key leaders
               form community board
                    │
                    Event— community board
                    risk assessment training
                    ├ - - - - - - - - - - - ┤
                    4. Community board
                       conducts risk assessment 1
                            │
                            Event— action planning/element fair
                            ├ - - - - - - - - - - - - - - - ┤
                            5. Board develops action plan
                               and task forces
```

In step 5, training should be scheduled for each of the specific program elements selected for implementation as part of the community's risk reduction plan. Program element training may range from large-group, generalized workshops at central locations to on-site training tailored specifically for service providers who will implement new programs.

As the communitywide program becomes more established, the community board should consider ways of expanding and institutionalizing the program. The community might consider establishing the board as an independent, nonprofit organization for communitywide coordination of drug abuse programs or setting up interagency agreements linking branches of local government or agencies that have a responsibility for youth, family, and drug abuse issues. For example, a "joint powers agreement" could be established for drug abuse prevention,

Figure 3.1. Timelines for Initiating Communities That Care, Cont'd.

Timeline for Phase II (Year 2)

Months

12	13	14	15	16	17	18	19	20	21	22	23	24	25

├ – – ┤

S 6. On-site technical assistance (T.A.)
T   to select final program elements
E   and plan implementation timeline
P   ├ – – ┤

      7. Task force augmentation in each element
        │
        8. Evaluation workshop
        ├ – – – – – ┤
        9. Training of
          appropriate community implementors
          for each program element
              ├ –
            10. Program element implementation
                      ├ – – – – – – – – – – – – – – – ┤
                      11. On-site T.A. to assist
                        with implementation
                        ├ – – – – – – – ┤
                        12. On-site T.A.
                        to plan for year 3
                        training needs

signed by the mayor's office, the police department, and the school system.

Sustaining the energy of a community board over a long period of time can be a challenge. Here are some ways to keep the spirit alive:

- Start small and build on success — do not try to do too much in the beginning.
- Establish a task force focused explicitly on board maintenance and recruitment.
- Recruit new members as needed.
- Keep decision making open and democratic, but make specific areas of responsibility clear.
- Avoid letting any individual dominate the board.

Figure 3.1. Timelines for Initiating Communities That Care, Cont'd.

Timeline for Phase II (Year 3)

Months

25	26	27	28	29	30	31	32	33	34	35	36

S
T
E
P

(Program element implementation continues)

⊢ – – ⊣
13. Additional training
    in each element

⊢ – – – – – – – – – – – – – – – ⊣
14. On-site T.A.
    on implementation issues

⊢ – – – – – – – – ⊣
15. Risk assessment 2

⊢ – – ⊣
16. On-site T.A.
    on planning year 4
    training needs

A Town Where It's Great to Be Born

To promote bonding in their community, one community board decided to set up a program that provided the family of every newborn child with a letter congratulating them on the birth and welcoming the new citizen to the town. Every year the family receives a letter with suggestions about positive parenting, books to read, and ways to promote the child's health and well-being.

Resources

For training, technical assistance, resource materials, and consultation on the "Communities That Care" community mobilization strategy, contact:

Developmental Research and Programs
130 Nickerson Street, Suite 107
Seattle, WA 98109
Phone: (800) 736-2630

Part Two

COMMUNITY ACTION
STRATEGIES

J. David Hawkins
Janet Y. Miller
Richard F. Catalano, Jr.

Chapter 4

Selecting the Best Approaches for Your Community

Armed with information on risks and resources in their communities, community boards must select new programs or strengthen existing programs to reduce risk and increase protective factors. Selecting specific programs that will reduce identified risk factors while increasing protective factors requires knowledge of a broad range of intervention approaches.

Part Two describes a number of promising approaches for risk reduction. These programs, all of which are grounded in reliable research, were included because they address risk factors for adolescent drug abuse and other problems *and* increase the protective factors against drug abuse specified in the social development strategy.

Taken as a set, the prevention approaches presented in these chapters describe a comprehensive model of risk reduction using the social development strategy. In communities where all of these approaches are in place, children are protected from risk, since they are bonded to their families, schools, and neighborhoods. They share the values of their communities and the larger society, and they seek health and achievement rather than the reinforcement of alcohol or other drugs.

Prevention groups using the "Communities That Care" process described earlier will, through a risk and resource assessment, identify elements of these programs already in place in their own communities. They will also identify areas of priority for risk reduction action. Having done so, they can use the following chapters to select prevention approaches that target the prioritized risk factors.

Every effort has been made to identify intervention concepts and specific program approaches that are solidly based in research and evaluation. A comprehensive review of programs known to be effective in reducing identified risk factors and strengthening protective factors has provided the basis for the selection (Hawkins et al., 1992). In some cases, specific programs are identified; in other cases more generic program approaches are described, within which several specific programs fit. For example, Chapter Six, "Early Childhood Education," outlines a general approach supported by numerous studies. Specific program components that have been linked to positive outcomes are noted, with guidelines to help community boards make their selections. Given the number of programs that have shown positive effects, no single program model is advocated for early childhood education. Chapter Twelve, "Media Mobilization," takes a similar approach, providing background information, national resources, and skills needed by community boards to work with local communications media in developing effective antidrug media campaigns. The campaign should be designed locally. In contrast, Chapters Seven and Eight, "Parent Training" and "School Organization and Management," describe specific, tested programs, with established content, procedures, and training strategies. This difference in specificity results from differences in the extent to which specific interventions for risk reduction have been developed and tested.

Certain principles govern the selection of any program. General criteria are offered here for selecting programs, along with a guide to the organization of the chapters and some thoughts on program training and evaluation.

"Communities That Care" aims at a coherent organization of intervention knowledge and identified risk and protective factors. Program elements have been included to represent a range of prevention approaches that meet the following five principles for preventive intervention:

1. Focus on reducing known risk factors by increasing known protective factors.
2. Address the risk factors at the appropriate developmental period, when they first become stable as predictors of dysfunction.
3. Intervene early, before drug use has started.
4. Include those at high risk by targeting high-risk individuals or high-risk community areas.
5. Address multiple risk factors in a comprehensive strategy.

Other programs not included here may meet these criteria. Community boards may wish to supplement this selection with other programs, and they should definitely review local programs already in place to determine how well they meet the five prevention principles. The five principles suggest the following five questions to ask in evaluating the promise of any prevention program.

1. *Does the program address known risk factors?* To prevent adolescent drug abuse, it is necessary to reduce factors that are predictive of adolescent drug abuse: "risk factors." Research has identified a number of risk factors—personal, social, and environmental conditions that predict a greater likelihood of drug abuse and other damaging adolescent behaviors. For example, school failure has been clearly identified as a risk factor not only for drug and alcohol abuse, but for other problems such as school dropout, delinquency, early pregnancy, and unemployment. In looking at the instructional skills programs described in Chapter Eleven, one can clearly see that they were designed to promote school success and reduce the likelihood of school failure, and that they have been effective in reaching those goals. It is in this way that community boards can take what is known about risk and protective factors and link that knowledge to prevention

programs. Each program element must meet the test of addressing specific, identified risk factors for adolescent drug abuse.

2. *How will the program reduce or eliminate the risk and increase protective factors?* Applying the social development strategy means choosing programs with a reasonable chance of reducing or eliminating risk in ways that promote protective factors against alcohol and other drug abuse. The program must lead to strengthened bonds with family, school, and other prosocial units that embody positive, antidrug norms. A prevention strategy must therefore have a demonstrated link both to reduction of risk and strengthening of bonds and clear standards for behavior. Where possible, this link should be substantiated by empirical research; if research is not available, the link must be theoretically sound.

3. *Does the program intervene at a developmentally appropriate time, before the targeted risk factors become stable predictors of problem behavior?* Prevention programs need to address risk factors at developmental points when they become reliable predictors of later drug problems, and before problems stabilize. Different risk factors are important at different points in child and adolescent development. For example, academic failure in grade four, five, or six is a predictor of later drug abuse. It is therefore important to ensure academic skill development in elementary school rather than waiting to intervene with intensive remediation programs when students are failing in later grades.

4. *Is the program likely to reach those individuals or groups at highest risk?* Prevention activities should be implemented in places where a large proportion of youngsters face risk factors such as family management problems, academic failure, neighborhood disorganization, and extreme economic and social deprivation. Important considerations should be weighed when deciding how to reach high-risk youngsters. Programs targeted only at individuals thought to be at risk may take on a stigma, since they are perceived to exist only for those who have problems. A related concern with individually targeted programs is the danger of labeling young children as future drug abusers by aiming a program exclusively at those exposed to early risk factors. In contrast, prevention programs located in areas with high concentrations of known risk factors can be offered to all those in

the targeted area, with the knowledge that a large proportion of children receiving the intervention are at risk and could benefit.

5. *Does the program address multiple risk factors in multiple domains (community, family, school, and individual/peer)?* No single program can address all risk factors. A single-focus strategy will not have much effect on the drug abuse problem. To maximize effects, prevention planners must put together a set of programs that cut across several areas of risk, integrate services across traditional boundaries, and provide risk reduction strategies across the continuum of development.

How the Program Elements Are Presented

The chapters in Part Two are all organized along parallel lines, although the program descriptions vary in important respects. These chapters are structured to provide readily accessible program information (1) to support new community initiatives targeting prioritized risk factors and (2) to provide a framework for assessing the relevance and adequacy of existing programs for reducing risks and increasing protective factors. Each chapter covers one program element, using a consistent structure of presentation.

Each chapter opens with a brief overview of the program element, which ties it to risk-focused prevention. Included in the synopsis are a brief description of the program and information on the appropriate age or developmental level and situation for its application and the problems/risk factors and protective factors it addresses. The remainder of the chapter is organized into the following sections:

- *Setting the Stage* provides a more detailed description of the program element.
- *Rationale* makes the case for including this particular program element.
- *Goals and Objectives* provides measurable targets for the intervention.
- *Supporting Research* summarizes the research studies that support the program element.

- *Program Description* details the program components and the steps necessary to carry them out.
- *Implementation* addresses issues of community readiness, support, and capacity required for success.
- *Training and Technical Assistance* estimates the training requirements of the program element, along with resource information for specific materials.
- *Evaluation* outlines approaches to assessing both process (Are we doing what we said we would do?) and outcomes (Is the program working?).
- *Resources* provides the names, addresses, and phone numbers of program sources.

It is important to recognize that successful implementation of any program element included in this book will require training and technical assistance. For most of the programs, specific training materials and workshops or training events have been developed and are available through the resources listed at the end of each chapter.

Program Evaluation

Program evaluation is fundamental to the "Communities That Care" community mobilization approach. Carefully documented process and outcome evaluation of programs is essential to guide future prevention efforts.

Many of the programs included here have developed specific evaluation tools, measures, and performance indicators. These, like training and technical assistance, are available by contacting the program developers.

To some extent, evaluation measures, like training and technical assistance, are specific to each program. In presenting each program element, we have identified considerations that should guide the development of both process and outcome evaluation of the program. However, two general comments apply to all program evaluation. First, the importance of evaluation cannot be overstated. The only way a community board can have confidence that an approach to drug abuse prevention is effective in its community is through careful evaluation and documentation of the approach taken and the outcomes achieved. To review our earlier discussion, the two basic evaluation questions of interest to a community board have to do with processes (what goes into the program's implementation) and outcomes (what are the program's effects). As we present each program element, we will frame the evaluation considerations around these two questions, offering samples of the kinds of process and outcome questions that apply to the particular program.

Second, it is important to incorporate evaluation questions into the initial conceptualization and planning of a program. All of the planning activities of the "Communities That Care" approach — identifying program goals and objectives and outlining strategies, timelines, and targets — imply evaluation questions. Designing the evaluation as part of the program planning process will help to ensure accountable processes, measurable objectives, and achievable outcomes. Evaluation should be an integral part of any prevention program. Its value is as great for program participants and service providers, answering their own questions about their activities and relationships, as it is for policy makers and researchers. Evaluation questions are the logical, natural extension of curiosity about what we are doing and whether it is having the effects we intend. Every effort should be made to make evaluation a practical, thoughtful observation and recording of processes, activities, and outcomes.

Kathryn E. Barnard   *Chapter 5*

Prenatal and Infancy Programs

Overview

Prenatal and infancy programs offer support and guidance to parents and their newborn at a very critical time of physical growth and psychological development. During pregnancy the health-promoting behaviors of a woman are important to the fetus; adequate nutrition and no ingestion of harmful substances (smoking, alcohol, illegal drugs) should be stressed. Prenatal medical care is important to healthy birth. After the baby is born, parents need continuing support and education about parenting and child development. Parents or infants at high risk need special services, including home visits by nurses and paraprofessionals. Promoting family attachment and positive parent-child interaction and bonding is a universal goal.

Prenatal and infancy programs that reduce risk while enhancing these protective factors include:

- *Prevention and Relationship Enhancement Program (PREP)*
- *Keys to Caregiving Videotape* series

- Public health nursing services
- Use of infant carriers
- Nursing Systems Toward Effective Parenting (Prenatal)
- Programs to address alcohol and drug use or addiction during and after pregnancy

The risk reduction programs described here target pregnant women, their partners, and their new infants through at least the first six months of life. All pregnant women need prenatal care and education for childbirth and later parenting. Parents with less than a high school education, adolescent parents, single parents, those with little social support, those who are misusing substances, and individuals with poor psychosocial functioning need more assistance. Prenatal care and education should be combined with outreach services through home visits or clinic-based contact with social workers, psychologists, or nutritionists.

Problems/risk factors addressed in this chapter are lack of prenatal care, preterm infants, poor family management practices (including child abuse or neglect), and family history of substance abuse.

Protective factors addressed in this chapter are parent-infant bonding and infant cognitive development.

Setting the Stage

Prevention can begin before a child is born. To prevent drug and alcohol abuse, programs need to start by ensuring a healthy infant and family. Today we have the knowledge and technology to achieve family planning and healthy babies, yet we are failing to provide community programs that support each pregnancy and enhance parenting skills (Children's Defense Fund, 1991; Miller, 1991; National Governors' Association Committee on Human Resources and Center for Policy Research, 1987; Public Health Service Expert Panel on the Content of Prenatal Care, 1989; Williams & Miller, 1991). It is estimated that up to half of urban newborns are at risk of later developmental and behavioral problems. The factors that put the newly born child at risk are maternal smoking (15 to 20 percent of pregnant women), drinking (57 percent), illegal drug use (11 percent), maternal age below twenty (12 percent), poverty (20 percent), and single parenthood (25 percent) (Chasnoff, Landress, & Barrett, 1990; Children's Defense Fund, 1991; Public Health Service Expert Panel on the Content of Prenatal Care, 1989; Streissguth et al., 1991; Zuckerman et al., 1989). Some of these factors also put the family at risk as a caregiving unit.

A dramatic change in an individual's or a couple's life takes place with the conception and birth of the first child. Having a healthy newborn is one of the best antecedents to successful parenting. Some communities have programs starting before marriage and pregnancy that also provide helpful instruction in couple communication (Markman, Duncan, Storaalski, & Howes, 1987; Markman & Kadushin, 1986). Nurturing a baby requires a great deal of energy and demands new skills. Even under the best conditions — two parents with a stable, happy relationship, adequate education, income, and housing — the task of the parent is daunting (Shanok, 1990). No longer do the adults control the family agenda; the newborn's need for food, comfort, and security determines everyone's sleep patterns and affects all aspects of family life, including a couple's relationship. The infant requires a growth-fostering environment — one in which the parent or adult caregiver is sensitive to the child's needs, responds to distress signals, and encourages social and cognitive growth (K. E. Barnard et al., 1989).

Research has shown that support for parents at the very beginning can influence the quality of parenting (D. E. Barnard, Booth, Mitchell, & Telzrow, 1988; K. E. Barnard et al., 1988; Weinraub & Wolf, 1983). Programs offering parent education and support exist in most communities. Prenatal education is often available through hospitals with maternity services, or through childbirth educators in the community at large. Through private or public prenatal medical care, a whole range of additional services are available, such as nursing, social work, nutrition counseling, and health education. These programs prepare the parent for the pregnancy, labor, and delivery but not necessarily for parenting the infant.

It seems obvious that the parent who does not have an

ideal situation needs parenting support even more. It is ironic that prenatal services, for example, are often less readily used by women who are unmarried, adolescent, depressed, misusing substances, or in general lack support. Outreach services such as public health nurses, school nurses, teachers, and drug counselors are important in identifying the parent's need and matching that need with community resources. An unmarried mother may prefer a prenatal education program for single mothers, or she may wish to have a coach who attends prenatal classes with her and provides support during labor and delivery.

Parent guidance and support after the baby is born are vital. Many parents have traditional well-child care from physicians or nurse health practitioners. Communities may also have parent groups sponsored by family-life programs in colleges and universities. These parent groups provide information about nurturing the growth and development of children and offer networks of parent peer support. Parents in contemporary society may have had little opportunity to learn the parenting role in their own families, since most families have a small number of children who are born within just a few years of each other. Today's parents are changing diapers, taking temperatures, soothing fussy babies, and teaching them about the world for the first time.

As with prenatal parent programs, high-risk parents need support and education programs tailored to their needs. A helping relationship may need to be established before information or more general support can be offered. Programs have been developed and tested that demonstrate effective outreach to high-risk parents (Anisfeld & Pincus, 1987; D. E. Barnard et al., 1988; K. E. Barnard et al., 1985; K. E. Barnard et al., 1988; Infant Health and Development Program, 1990; Olds, Henderson, Chamberlin, & Tatelbaum, 1986; U.S. General Accounting Office, 1990).

Several existing organizations provide training and technical assistance in prenatal and infancy programs. Organizations listed in the Resources section at the end of this chapter can link community boards with program developers and consultants to help in planning and implementing this program element.

Rationale

Evidence suggests that the child's development of a sense of security is one of the strongest influences in determining later developmental course and success in school (Greenberg, Cicchette, & Cummings, 1990; Morisset, Barnard, Greenberg, Booth, & Spieker, 1990; Stroufe, 1983). Children develop a sense of security in the early days, weeks, and months of life if they have a caregiver who responds to them (Ainsworth, Behar, Water, & Wall, 1978).

A sensitive caregiver monitors the infant's behavior and responds to behavioral cues of need. This is the mechanism through which the child develops a secure attachment to the parent or other caregiver (Morisset et al., 1990; Tronick, 1989). A skilled caregiver in close physical contact with a baby knows when the baby is hungry, tired, or bored before the baby has a chance to cry.

Healthy newborns who are born on time and are of average weight are more likely to be good cue givers. Infants born preterm and infants influenced by maternal substance abuse during pregnancy are likely to have body language that is muted or confusing to the caregiver (K. E. Barnard et al., 1989; Chasnoff, Griffith, MacGregor, Dirkes, & Burns, 1989). These high-risk babies are also likely to be more unpredictable in sleeping schedules, fussier, and harder to feed. Follow-up studies reveal that with complications of pregnancy, labor, and delivery, high-risk infants are particularly sensitive to the postnatal environment. With good parenting, even these problems are less likely to influence the child's subsequent developmental course (Ramey et al., in press). In summary,

- Parents' emotional distress and lack of interpersonal, educational, and financial resources constitute potent risk factors for their children in terms of intellectual delay, school failure, and child psychopathology (Morisset et al., 1990; Rutter, 1985; Sameroff & Emde, 1990; Sameroff & Seifer, 1983).
- Infant biological factors such as preterm birth, small birth-

weight for age, or prenatal alcohol or drug exposure constitute potent risk factors for intellectual delay, school failure, and child psychopathology (Chasnoff, 1991; Howard, Beckwith, Rodning, & Kropenske, 1989; Infant Health and Development Program, 1990; Rutter, 1985).

- Parent-infant interaction and attachment influence the child's developmental course. Secure attachment can modify the influence of high-risk environments on the child's intellectual outcome, language skill, and school performance (K. E. Barnard et al., 1989; Greenberg et al., 1990; Morisset et al., 1990; Ramey, Farran, & Campbell, 1978; Stroufe, 1983).
- Establishing positive, growth-promoting parent-infant communication is the most important foundation for the emotional and intellectual development of the child (Bee et al., 1982; Bruner, 1981; Howlin & Rutter, 1987).

Goals and Objectives

Goals

- To promote the birth of a healthy infant
- To promote parent-infant bonding and positive parent-infant interaction
- To promote parental strategies that foster social and cognitive growth
- To reduce family conflict especially pertaining to child care
- To reduce abusive and neglectful child-care practices

Objectives

- To increase positive and supportive communication between the parents
- To increase health-promoting behaviors of the mother during her pregnancy and breast feeding
- To increase parental knowledge about infant behavior and growth-fostering parental strategies
- To increase secure attachment of the infant to the parent or primary caregiver

Supporting Research

During the past twenty-five years, knowledge has grown about risk and protective factors for early development. Numerous longitudinal studies of infants and children have demonstrated the influence of the family environment on the child's development (Rutter, 1987).

Prenatal Care

Studies indicate that starting the world as a full-term, average-weight baby with no respiratory difficulty and free from infections is ideal. Evidence provides confirmation that obtaining prenatal care before the last three months of pregnancy is associated with better infant outcomes. The exact mechanism is uncertain; is it something magical about medical care or is it the nature of the mother who seeks out preventive health care services? The truth undoubtedly lies somewhere in between. Nevertheless, an important goal of any community is to ensure prenatal care to all pregnant women as early in pregnancy as possible and certainly before the third trimester. Ideally, women should prepare for pregnancy with good nutrition and healthful behaviors before conception (Public Health Service Expert Panel on the Content of Prenatal Care, 1989).

Too many pregnant women do not seek early prenatal care. There are many reasons for this. There may be cultural factors that encourage seeing pregnancy as a normal, healthy state that requires no doctor. If the mother is undecided about whether to continue the pregnancy, she may delay seeing any health provider until she makes her decision. Women of low income and little education may be particularly reluctant to seek care from unfamiliar, potentially unfriendly health care providers.

Fortunately, there are now federally supported and mandated programs in most states that foster a full range of friendly, helpful prenatal services and that reimburse private physicians, nurses, nutritionists, and social workers for providing care for low-income families. These state programs are called *Improved Pregnancy Outcome programs,* and each state and county health office can readily explain what local community services are available for prenatal care. In addition to medical care, there should be services to support smoking cessation, to foster alcohol and illegal drug avoidance, and to address occupational and environmental and health concerns. Pregnant women need services to improve psychological well-being and help with problems of domestic violence, psychiatric illness, and stress and anxiety. Services to improve nutritional status — including nutritional assessment and food supplementation for those who cannot afford to buy the food they need — are especially important.

Drug and alcohol treatment programs designed to serve pregnant women and mothers and their children have only recently been available. Experience to date is limited, but they seem to be effective in reducing the drug or alcohol use among those women who seek such care; the major problem is that substance-abusing women often are in a poor health state prior to pregnancy and do not seek prenatal care until complications occur or they are late in pregnancy. Earlier prevention of substance use with school-age and adolescent children and for all women of reproductive age is the ultimate goal.

> Educational programs on substance use and abuse in pregnancy must be initiated on two fronts: public and professional. The public must be made to understand that any substance use by a woman of childbearing age can place an unborn child at risk, often before the woman realizes she is pregnant. Professional education must focus on history taking skills for substance abuse and appropriate use of urine and blood toxicologies within the overall clinical realm. The most commonly missed diagnosis in obstetric and pediatric medicine is maternal drug use in pregnancy, yet the long-term health and welfare of the children are at the greatest risk [Chasnoff, 1991, p. 43].

In recent years, preparing for childbirth has become the focus of prenatal education classes. Most programs consist of six to nine classes that provide information about the normal course of pregnancy and prepare the woman and her partner to manage labor and delivery. The couples gain confidence and see the importance of teamwork as the partner learns to coach the pregnant woman through her labor and delivery. This emphasis on teamwork has other benefits as well: it has been shown that couples in Lamaze childbirth education classes demonstrated more satisfaction with their relationship after the child's birth than did parents without Lamaze training (Markman & Kadushin, 1986).

Growth-Fostering Parenting in the First Year

The developmental tasks of the infant and young child provide the context for parenting. During the first months of life, the infant is learning to regulate all body systems. The baby is learning how to process sights, sounds, textures, and smells and how to regulate her responses to the environment. Patterns of sleep and feeding are emerging as well as small, subtle responses to caregiving. The child learns to become soothed when comforted, and this is an important developmental milestone. The caregiver learns what distinct cries mean, how the baby will respond to changes in caregiving routine, and so on, and these are all important lessons (Fraiberg, 1980; Greenspan & Lourie, 1981). Physical contact with the baby, such as carrying the baby in a soft front pack like a Snugli, helps the caregiver respond immediately to any change in the infant's activity, which reduces crying and satisfies the infant's need for responsive caregiving.

Around three or four months of age, the baby becomes a very social creature. Any adult who acts playful may be rewarded with a social smile. Games of peek-a-boo and patty-cake show off the baby's personality, as the infant learns the give and take of communication. Long, intent gazes and wide, full-face smiles provide tremendous positive feedback to the caregiver. An infant needs a lot of face-to-face interaction, social games, and talking to — the baby becomes the main family entertainment. At this age, a baby is dependent on the adult caregiver for most experience of the environment; without locomotion or efficient hand function, the baby has contact only with what the parent facilitates (Bradley, 1987).

Around seven or eight months of age, the child will start becoming more demanding and will want to do things like self-feeding. The infant will begin pointing a finger to indicate demands. Soon a marvelous burst of language and locomotion will transform the child's world. All during these early months, the child has been developing a sense of trust in the larger environment. The parent has responded first to basic needs: feeding the baby, offering comfort and support, and providing fun when he or she is ready to explore the world. With a sense of security the child is now ready to explore, to move on all fours, and soon to walk and talk. Now the child is better equipped to elicit responses from caregivers, and parenting improves even for children in the most high-risk social environments.

Parents who were not well nurtured themselves are likely to have difficulty in this early caregiving stage. Some indicators are lack of high school completion, insufficient income, being under eighteen years of age, alcohol or drug use, mental retardation, mental illness such as depression, and lack of support networks. Difficult life circumstances such as trouble with the law, outstanding loans, moving, family arguments, illnesses in the family, drug or alcohol use by household members, and abusive relationships, to name a few, make parenting more difficult (K. E. Barnard, 1989; Mercer, 1990; Spieker & Booth, 1988; Tableman & Katzenmeyer, 1985).

Support for high-risk parents is critical. Effective programs have shown the need for sustained and frequent contact beginning as early as possible during pregnancy and continuing until the child's second year. Often such programs of outreach are provided by community health nurses or paraprofessionals. The first step is developing a trusting relationship with the parents, who must come to trust the intervener as someone they can count on to be interested and to help address life's daily issues. Once the relationship is established, parents will be open to information and help. As the parent learns to trust the helper, the infant has a better chance to develop essential trust in the parent (K. E. Barnard et al., 1985; K. E. Barnard et al., 1988; Cicchette

& Toth, 1987; Larner & Halpern, 1987; Musick, Bernstein, Percansky, & Stott, 1987).

Program Description

Preventive programs aimed at improving the outcome of pregnancy and of the parenting environment are generally found in health-related service agencies. Prenatal care is based in the medical services. Prenatal education may be offered in hospitals, private educational services, or medical clinics. Well-child care is based generally in health services. Parent groups may be developed in many settings. Home outreach to families is a public health or nursing service. Prenatal and postpartum classes associated with hospitals, health maintenance organizations, and other groups are an important resource for the pregnant and parenting woman and her partner.

The key protective functions of prenatal and postpartum family and child services are summarized here.

Prenatal Services

- Promote adequate nutrition for the pregnant woman.
- Provide both adequate monitoring of and knowledge about physical and emotional changes during pregnancy and fetal development.
- Encourage the woman to improve or maintain behaviors that promote both the fetus's health and her own.
- Prepare the woman and her partner for the process of labor and birth.
- Promote the emotional well-being of the woman and her unborn child.
- Promote the development of a parenting role, including bonding to the baby during pregnancy.
- Reinforce or build commitment of support systems.

Family and Child Services

- Promote the capacity of the parents to provide optimal care for the infant.

- Reduce family stresses.
- Promote the attachment of the parent to the infant and of the infant to the parent.
- Promote the physical and emotional well-being of the parent and the infant.

Relationship Enhancement Training

The *Prevention and Relationship Enhancement Program (PREP)* offers an effective means to enrich the capacity for parenting an infant. Teaching communication skills and the management of emotions is the focus of a relationship enhancement program for couples to counteract known or suspected causes of marital and family distress and enhance couples' abilities to develop and maintain intimacy. When families are stressed, effective communication becomes even more important. Videotapes are available for teaching couples effective communication skills from the Center for Marital and Family Studies, University of Denver (see the Resources section at the end of this chapter).

Keys to Caregiving Videotape Series

This educational videotape series on early infant care covers infant state, infant behaviors, parent-infant interaction, and infant state modulation. The series was designed for hospital nurses to increase their effectiveness in educating parents about their newborn and in particular in introducing new parents to their infant's capacity for responding to them and to the environment. This is an excellent inservice program for hospitals and community health nursing agencies (produced by NCAST Publications, University of Washington—see the Resources).

Public Health Nursing Service

This resource should be available in communities, although tight state and local budgets have tended to limit it to clients with the highest medical or social risks.

A number of resources are available to guide the public

health nurse making home visits to childbearing families. One such guide is a set of protocols developed by nurses at the University of Washington and the Seattle–King County Health Department (Kang, Rollolazo, Yoshihara, & Thibodeaux, 1989). For the prenatal period, the protocol covers six contacts. The first contacts take place as soon as possible after the woman becomes aware she is pregnant and include access to prenatal care, dietary assessment and advice, genetic screening, and recommendations to avoid harmful substances. During the pregnancy, the nurse visits monthly and continues to monitor the woman's physical health and offer anticipatory advice about early labor, planning for labor and delivery, and preparing for the infant's care.

Postpartum nursing visits are suggested for at least the first six months, beginning at hospital discharge. These visits cover information on the care of the baby and the health and well-being of the mother, specifically infant feeding and nutrition, parent-child interaction, monitoring the infant's growth and development, and dealing with crying. Protocols are developed for the content and process of these nursing visits (K. E. Barnard, 1991).

Promoting the Use of Infant Carriers

Research shows that the ideal situation for the infant and mother is to be in close physical proximity in the earliest months of life (Anisfeld, Casper, Nozyce, & Cunningham, 1990). This is consistent with "attachment theory," which hypothesizes that infants need a sense of security from the caregiver when they are at their most helpless — cannot yet talk or get around on their own. This thinking and research supports the idea of promoting the use of infant carriers, like the Snugli, as a community program.

In an experimental study, Anisfeld and her group assigned low-income mothers to two conditions: one condition was provision of the Snugli and the other, provision of a common infant seat where the baby could be safely put down by the mother. The mothers were free to use the devices as they chose. At two months, 86 percent of the Snugli mothers were using the device; at thirteen months, approximately 48 percent were using it daily,

48 percent two or three times a week, and 4 percent less than two or three times a week. The infant seats had higher use, with 92 percent reporting use at two months; at thirteen months, 72 percent of the mothers used the infant seat daily.

Mother-child interaction was measured at three months and attachment security at thirteen months. Mothers using the Snugli at three months were found to be more responsive to their infants than the mothers using infant seats, and at thirteen months the Snugli infants were more securely attached to their mothers (83 percent versus 38 percent). The results are positive and suggest that for low-income, inner city mothers, a baby carrier promotes more physical contact with the infant. The baby carrier puts the mother and baby in a context where the mother can be fully aware of her infant and the infant can easily cue her mother. Further replications of the Snugli study are in process, but the need for early proximity of caregiver and infant is so well grounded in attachment theory that this intervention seems one that should be encouraged. Two considerations: (1) choose a soft body sling or pack that is safe for carrying the infant and comfortable for the mother, and (2) assess whether the mother has any aversion to body contact with the infant, which could elicit negative responses from the closely held infant.

Nursing Systems Toward Effective Parenting (Preterm)

This prevention/intervention home visit program is designed to support the adaptation between the parent and preterm infant. The program was developed under my direction to assist parents in learning how to manage their preterm infant after hospital discharge. The overall goal is the development of a therapeutic relationship with the parent(s) in which health-related concerns, state modulation, parent-infant interaction, the infant's environment, and parental coping are dealt with. The program has proven effective with preterm infants and has also been used to cope with the behavioral responses of infants affected by prenatal drug use (see NCAST Publications in the Resources section).

Programs That Address Addiction in Pregnancy

Special programs for women who are addicted and who are pregnant or have young children are now being offered by more communities. Services range from clinics that provide both drug treatment and pregnancy or well-child care to residential drug treatment programs for women and children. The effectiveness of the programs varies. Aims are to reduce the use of drugs and to promote a healthy pregnancy and baby (Weston, Ivins, Zuckerman, Jones, & Lopez, 1990).

Implementation

Community groups that, through a risk and resource assessment of their communities, have identified as priorities maternal alcohol or other drug use during pregnancy, unacceptable numbers of preterm and low-birthweight infants, or poor early parenting practices should establish a prenatal and infancy program task force.

This task force will work with public health officials and primary care providers to plan for the expansion of prenatal and infancy programs to currently underserved populations at risk. Representatives of local community health agencies; local teaching and public health hospitals; private practitioners; and the professional associations of nurses, physicians, and related health professions should be included in the task force to facilitate the implementation of initiatives to provide both prenatal care and education about childbirth and parenting for all women in the community.

Training and Technical Assistance

Training and technical assistance will be needed for communities initiating prenatal and infancy programs and should be sought locally through the Resources listed at the end of the chapter.

Evaluation

Process Evaluation

Strong emphasis is placed on assessment of whether communities have the range of prenatal and postpartum medical, educational, and outreach services needed. Also important is the extent to which high-risk individuals in the community are receiving care. If many are not, then barriers to care need to be assessed. Areas to assess in process evaluation include the following:

- Percent of pregnant women receiving prenatal care prior to the third trimester
- Availability of prenatal and postpartum educational classes
- Percent of the "at-risk" population served with outreach and follow-through contacts
- Content of prenatal and parenting classes to ensure that material on relationships — marital/partner and parent-child — is included

Outcome Evaluation

The following goals form the basis for outcome evaluation of prenatal and infant programs:

- Ninety-five percent of pregnant women receive early prenatal care.
- Less than 7 percent of infants are born preterm.
- Less than 25 percent of couples expecting children report marital distress.
- Fewer pregnant women use alcohol (less than 50 percent).
- Fewer pregnant women use illegal drugs (less than 10 percent).
- Establishment of positive parent-child interaction.
- Low rates of child abuse.
- Seventy-five percent or more of the children have secure attachment.

Pregnancy and early infancy involve transitions of roles for new parents. Behavioral changes can often occur more easily at times of major life and role transitions. Therefore, the period of time surrounding conception, pregnancy, and first parenting is ideal for initiating positive behavioral change related to smoking, alcohol, and drug use.

Resources

The Perinatal Resource Center studies and reviews policies and provides interdisciplinary training in the field of perinatal substance abuse and its prevention. For further information, contact:
Office of Substance Abuse Prevention
Perinatal Resource Center
Dr. Milton Lee, Director
9300 Lee Highway
Fairfax, VA 22031
Phone: (202) 842-8905

For more information on relationship enhancement training, contact:
Prevention and Relationship Enhancement Program (PREP)
PREP Educational Videos, Inc.
Dr. Howard J. Markman, Director
Center for Marital and Family Studies
University of Denver
Denver, CO 80028
Phone: (800) 366-0166

NCAST Publications produces the *Keys to Caregiving* videotape series discussed in this chapter. For more information, contact:
NCAST Publications
University of Washington, WJ-10
Seattle, WA 98195
Phone: (206) 543-8528

Chapter 6

Early Childhood Education

Overview

Early childhood education programs offer support for parents and children at a critical point in children's lives: the preschool years. Successful completion of early developmental tasks has an important impact on children's later social and cognitive growth and school adjustment. The programs included here, designed for home or center/school settings, focus on two important aspects of child development, both related to later school success: reading readiness and developing self-control.

Programs that reduce risk by enhancing protective factors through home-based approaches are:

- The Mother-Child Home Program of the Verbal Interaction Project
- Problem-Solving Techniques in Childrearing
- Book lending libraries

Center or school-based programs:

- Preschool programs to develop language skills (DISTAR; High/Scope Cognitive Curriculum; STaR)
- Reading programs for reading-ready children (phonics-based and whole-language approaches)

Early childhood programs serve children from two to five years of age and their parents. Some of the families who especially need support during the preschool years are those headed by single parents, who may be teenaged and may live in poverty.

Problems/risk factors addressed in this chapter are poor family management practices, academic failure, early antisocial behavior, and low commitment to school.

Protective factors addressed in this chapter are bonding to family and school, cognitive and social skill development, self-control skills, and opportunities for developmentally appropriate interactions.

Setting the Stage

"As the twig is bent, so grows the tree." This old adage sums up what volumes of research and decades of studies have told us repeatedly about high-risk youth: problem behaviors like drug abuse and delinquency start to develop early in a child's life. The sooner the risk factors for these behaviors can be identified and prevented or their effects diminished, the better a child's chances will be of leading a healthy, successful life later on.

Early childhood education provides support for children and their parents between the ages of two and five, before the children begin elementary school. This program element emphasizes support not just for the children but also for their parents, so that the whole family can help their children become competent and successful as they make the crucial transition to elementary school.

Replicated studies have shown that early education programs, like the ones described in this chapter, can be a key factor in promoting children's later success in school and life. When considering this program element, however, remember that research has also shown that the benefits of early childhood education programs fade unless followed by high-quality educational programs — programs like those described in late chapters of this book.

Rationale

Early school failure can be crippling to a child, and it may be difficult or impossible to catch up later on. Early school problems are widespread among low-income and racial/ethnic minority youth, and the effects are particularly devastating for them. In one typical urban school district in the spring of 1987, 18 percent of first-grade students were retained — required to repeat the grade — because they had not been able to learn the first-grade material. The next year 20 percent were kept back. Race and gender figure largely in these numbers: in this same district, the first-grade retention rate for African-American males was 1.7 times higher than for European-American females.

Troublesome behavior is closely related to early school failure. Between 4 and 10 percent of all children nationwide are classified as having what psychologists and psychiatrists call "conduct disorders." A large proportion of children who later come before the courts and one-third to one-half of those involved in child and adolescent clinic referrals started out with conduct disorders (G. D. Gottfredson, 1987).

In studies that have traced how early school failure and conduct disorders are connected to problems in adolescence, several patterns have emerged. Poor school performance and disruptive conduct contribute to placement in special education classes. This placement, in turn, narrows a child's social world to other children with problems, limiting opportunities to learn prosocial skills from peers. Special education placement may carry a long-lasting stigma. Being classified as an academic and social failure by those in positions of authority may shape a child's self-perception of competence, which determines future effort. Early school failure often translates into a child's lowered expectations for success in school, and low expectations may lead to delinquency, drug use, dropping out, and similar problems. A child's aggressiveness and lack of social skills, such as not knowing how to join a play group, can also lead to rejection by peers (Coie, Rabiner, & Lochman, 1989). The same behavior that results in peer rejection in the early grades is likely to result in rejection by prosocial peers in adolescence.

Early childhood education can help a child avoid these difficulties. Researchers in the Perry Preschool Project have reported the following lasting results for the nineteen-year-olds who had been part of their early childhood education program (Berrueta-Clement et al., 1984):

- Improved cognitive performance during early childhood
- Improved school placement and achievement during the school years
- Lower rates of delinquency and crime
- Decreased use of welfare assistance
- Lower incidence of teenage pregnancy
- Increased high school graduation rates
- Greater enrollment in postsecondary schooling and employment

Goals and Objectives

Goals

- To reduce poor family management practices, early antisocial behavior, academic failure, and low commitment to school
- To promote bonding to family and school, cognitive and social skill development, self-control skills, and opportunities for developmentally appropriate interactions

Objectives

- To increase involvement of high-risk parents and children in a variety of early risk reduction activities
- To increase high-risk children's social and academic preparedness for elementary school

Supporting Research

In the last three decades, significant strides have been made in the area of early childhood education. Much is now known about what does and does not work. To reduce academic failure and conduct problems in the early grades, we need to focus on two main aspects of children's behavior: reading readiness and self-control.

Reading Readiness

A wide range of language skills are needed by a child before learning to read. Children's reading readiness levels can be enhanced before they enter first grade by providing a language-enriched home environment and language-enriched preschool and kindergarten environments with reading instruction for children who are at the appropriate stage in their development (generally five years of age). As the National Institute of Education's *Becoming a Nation of Readers* (1985, p. 21) points out, "Reading begins in the home. To a greater or lesser degree, depending upon the home, children acquire knowledge before coming to school that lays the foundation for reading. They acquire concepts for understanding things, events, thoughts, and feelings, and the oral language vocabulary for expressing these concepts. They acquire the basic grammar of oral language."

Parents play an important role in preparing children to read. The amount of time parents spend reading with their children is one of the clearest predictors of early reading ability (Mason & Allen, 1986). Besides simply reading to their children, parents can help by providing a language-enriched home environment. This means emphasizing the role of language in everything we do — pointing out letters, signs, and labels, for example, and giving children opportunities to read, spell, and print words before they start elementary school. Helping children to associate words with familiar signs or labels stimulates reading by making them aware of printed language and giving them experience in learning letters and sounding out words.

Parents can do specific things that can help their children

learn to read and write. Children are better prepared for reading when their parents help them move from understanding words in context (like labels and signs) to understanding words out of context (for example, words in isolation or sentences in books whose meaning is not given by pictures). Having books in the home is also important. And the complexity of the stories a parent reads and even the way a parent reads to a child can make a difference. For example, parents can ask thought-provoking questions that do not have simple, one-word answers. Encouraging a child to tell a story in his or her own words is also helpful.

The National Institute of Education's *Becoming a Nation of Readers* (1985) stresses that nonreading experiences are also important for learning to read. Even simple stories call on the child's store of knowledge about the world. The child who has been to the zoo, for example, will find it much easier to read and understand a story about the zoo or about animals. Talking to children about a new experience is also important, to help them understand it and be able to draw on the experience later on.

Reducing Problem Behavior

Reducing problem behavior means teaching children self-control. One approach to reducing children's problem behavior is for adults to establish clear rules, monitor and supervise the child's behavior, consistently enforce rules, and reinforce desired behavior. These principles can be effective when applied both at home and in the classroom. Approaches that focus exclusively on adult control of children's behavior may be harmful in the long run, however, because they fail to develop the child's ability to control his or her own behavior. Child development experts now widely agree that self-monitoring is more effective than external monitoring for controlling behavior.

Helping children learn how to solve problems and resolve conflicts is a more child-centered form of behavior management that complements the clear establishment and monitoring of rules. This approach teaches children such skills as stopping to think about what they are doing instead of behaving impulsively, considering alternative solutions to problems, predicting the consequences of alternative solutions, and considering the effects of their behavior on others.

These are complex skills for young children. Often it is necessary first to teach children much simpler skills such as understanding explanations that involve the concepts of "if . . . then . . . " and "same" and "different." Other skills children should learn in a preschool program (or at home) have to do with feelings — understanding and naming them. Once children have learned these skills, they are ready for problem-solving exercises that might use puppet role plays or discussions of problem situations. Activities and exercises to stimulate children's learning of problem-solving skills have been developed for preschool and kindergarten teachers and for parents to use at home. Home-based programs are similar to school- or child center-based programs. They require the parent to set aside a certain period of time (twenty minutes or so) every day for specific activities and interaction with the child aimed at developing self-control skills. Home visits can be important in encouraging and helping parents to find time for these activities with their young children.

Another approach that can improve children's behavior and self-control is to focus on increasing secure attachments or bonds to parents. Families characterized by warmth and acceptance, parental responsiveness, flexibility, and the use of clear-cut expectations have more securely attached children who later — in preschool — are more popular, engage more frequently in social contact, and are more effective in helping others (Hartup, 1989). These features of family interactions have been shown to predict school readiness on entry to first grade and school achievement in later years (Estrada, Arsenio, Hess, & Holloway, 1987).

Developmental Appropriateness

Whether at school or at home, early childhood education must be developmentally appropriate, sensitive to the child's needs and individual readiness to learn specific social or academic skills.

This contrasts with programs or frameworks that assume all children should be learning the same kinds of skills at the same time. For preschool children, *active learning* is a key concept. Children at this stage tend to learn through physical involvement with objects and the environment around them. They are just beginning to be able to reflect on their own actions, solve abstract problems, and distinguish symbolic representations from the things they stand for (Hohmann, Banet, & Weikart, 1979). All of these aspects of children's development need to be taken into account when planning early childhood programs to promote social and cognitive development.

Program Description

An effective early childhood education program should take place both at home and in a preschool child center or kindergarten. Both parent education and the center-based preschool/kindergarten program should promote language skills; increase clarity of rules, consistency of enforcement of rules, and consequences for behavior; and increase the child's self-management skills. In addition, the center-based program will begin to teach reading skills for students who are ready to learn to read, and the parents will learn to increase family bonding and attachment between themselves and their children.

These two components — home and center — complement each other and have similar goals. The main difference is that the home component focuses on providing training and support to parents, primarily in the home setting, and the center/school component provides training and support to teachers and other child-care professionals. Following are descriptions of a variety of programs, approaches, and strategies that have been used effectively in the two settings.

Parent Programs and Approaches

The *Mother-Child Home Program of the Verbal Interaction Project* focuses on trained "toy demonstrators" who conduct weekly or semiweekly home play sessions involving the mother and child together. Specially designed materials are used to stimulate verbal interaction. The program aims at strengthening positive interaction between the parent and child, improving the child's language skills, and helping the parent support the child's social and emotional development (Levenstein, O'Hara, & Madden, 1983).

Problem-Solving Techniques in Childrearing, aimed at mothers of young children, focuses on verbal interaction between the mother and child, encouraging questioning by the mother and expression by the child. It teaches parents to discipline their children through a problem-solving approach. The core of the program is a series of problem-solving games the mother and child play together. Here is one example.

> Now this is just a game. *Have each child hold a toy previously used from trinket box.* Peter, you snatch Kevin's toy from him.
>
> Kevin, how do you feel about that? *Kevin responds.*
>
> Peter, now let him have it back.
>
> Now how do you feel, Kevin? *After child answers repeat with other pairs . . .*
>
> Let's pretend someone came along and threw [a] ball out the window so Steven could not play with it anymore. Now how do you think Steven might feel?
>
> He might feel sad or he might feel mad. How can we find out? *Encourage children to ask* [Spivack, Platt, & Shure, 1976, p. 183].

Scripts for the games present a series of increasingly difficult problems to solve and ask the child to suggest solutions, potential consequences of the solutions, and pairing of specific consequences with specific solutions. The scripts also focus on developing language skills, gathering information (through such questions as "How can we tell?"), and identifying and labeling one's own and others' emotions (Spivack et al., 1976). Spivack et al. (1976, p. 203) offer the following example of an exercise meant to foster children's understanding of emotions.

This part of the script stresses how to understand and influence others' emotions. For mothers playing with one child, puppets are used as a substitute for other children. For example, the mother holds up the puppet (Terry) and follows with: "Let's make up a story. Let's pretend we know that Terry likes cookies. If you let him have a cookie, would that make Terry happy?" After the child answers, the puppet is asked if he would be happy if the child gave him a cookie. Terry answers yes.

Then the mother asks how Terry might feel "if you would *not* let him have a cookie." After the child answers, Terry says, "Yes, that would make me mad (or sad)." The purpose is to get the child to think through the influence of specific actions on others' feelings.

Offering a book lending library — simply giving favorite books to children to take home and advising the parents about ways to help their children learn to read — appears to be effective in developing prereading skills (McCormick & Mason, 1987).

Center-Based Programs and Approaches

A variety of center-based approaches have been effective in developing the language skills of preschool children and preparing them for successful entry into the primary grades. In one highly structured approach, the Bereiter-Englemann/DISTAR model, the teacher models the correct use of language and elicits correct responses from children (Carnine, Carnine, Karp, & Weisberg, 1988). Using another approach, the *High/Scope Cognitive Curriculum,* the teacher divides the classroom into language-oriented learning centers that encourage children to use, experience, and discover language through activities and play (Berrueta-Clement et al., 1984). The following account of a visit to a Head Start preschool illustrates this approach:

> I joined a teacher engaged with five children at a low table, planning the morning's activities. The teacher, Ms. Brownlee, talked with each child in turn about his or her choice of activities and work area—arts, blocks, housekeeping, music, sand, or quiet games. I was impressed with how the teacher responded to each child's choice, sometimes helping the child to elaborate his plan, sometimes helping two children to make a plan together. Then the children went off, taking with them their individual signs (bearing name and Polaroid picture) to be hung in the chosen activity area. Soon the children were busy painting, doing puzzles, building with blocks, putting dolls to bed, or sending sand through sieves and funnels [Schorr, 1988, p. 199].

A third and highly interactive approach known as *STaR* involves the telling and retelling of stories. Children listen to a story, respond to questions about it, and then retell it in pairs and groups (Karweit, 1989b).

Many of the programs designed to develop language skills also focus on reading skills for four- and five-year-olds. Currently two contrasting approaches are favored. One, the phonics approach, is highly structured and teacher-directed. It breaks language down into sounds, which are then reconstructed into words and sentences. This approach has been successful in increasing learning among disadvantaged five-year-olds (Carnine et al., 1988). The other is the whole-language approach, which emphasizes the "natural" use of language in everyday settings (sending notes and messages, reading and writing that meets specific, practical needs). The two philosophies lead to very different kinds of activities in the classroom, yet research suggests that both approaches can be effective. Programs based on the differing philosophies do have in common the use of a clear structure of specific materials, management plans, and activities. Ample experience with oral and printed language is what the child who is not yet ready to read needs most.

A "daily report card" system has been effective in changing young children's problem behavior. This involves setting clear standards for behavior, keeping a daily log (the report card) noting each time the child follows the rules for a fixed period of time and rewarding the child with specific privileges at home or school. Such an approach can be used for both social and academic problem behaviors.

Similar to the home-based problem-solving approach for parents described earlier, *Interpersonal Cognitive Problem-Solving* provides teachers with a script composed of thirty-five games that help to develop thinking and problem-solving skills in children. Through enactment and discussion of the games, the children are encouraged to respond with solutions to the problems presented, state consequences of these solutions, and pair specific solutions with specific consequences. A strong emphasis is placed on the language skills needed for thinking about solutions, consequences, and alternatives. As with the home-based version of this program, the children also learn to identify and label emotions as part of solving conflicts and problems (Spivack et al., 1976).

Implementation

Context

A major consideration in implementing preschool programs is context. Recent studies showing long-term effects of preschool programs have led some to think preschool is the "silver bullet" that will cure all educational ills. The majority of studies do show consistent early gains for preschool youngsters (Lazar, Darlington, Murray, Royce, & Snipper, 1982), but these advantages "fade out" by about second grade. The benefits of preschool are real and important; nevertheless, high-quality educational and social skill development programs are needed throughout a child's school career to maintain early advantages. Community boards considering this program element should view it in the broader context of approaches that will sustain the positive effects of preschool programs over time.

Most early childhood education programs offered by public agencies operate for less than three and one-half hours per day. A hotly debated issue is whether programs should operate on a full school-day schedule (five to six hours) or an extended day schedule that would match parents' work schedules. The major benefit of shorter days is their lower cost. Arguments for full-day programs cite their convenience for parents, more time for instruction and other activities, greater flexibility in programming, and reduction in the stress caused by moving children from setting to setting during the day. Although research suggests that disadvantaged students gain from a longer day, the evidence is not conclusive. The main point to keep in mind is that the length of the day should be sufficient to allow time for the program to be implemented effectively.

Selecting a Program

A wide variety of early education programs are available today, and there are significant differences among them. Some are academic, following a strictly defined curriculum; others are developmental, encouraging the teacher to take account of the child's readiness to learn specific skills. Some are teacher-directed, others student-centered and student-initiated. Some focus on the child, others on the family.

All these types of preschool and kindergarten programs have proven effective in producing higher test scores as well as fewer special education placements and less grade retention (Karweit, 1989a, 1989b, 1989c; Stallings & Stipek, 1986; Weiss, 1988). In fact, there is little evidence of the superiority of one program or approach to another. Nevertheless, it is possible to make some general recommendations based on the available research:

- Structured programs — those with a specific set of learning objectives and teaching methodologies — are more effective than unstructured programs such as nursery school models in which the child is encouraged to play freely.
- The program should include language-development oppor-

tunities, reading instruction for those who are ready, and social skill–building activities (Warger, 1988).

- Local professionals who have expertise in early childhood education and development and who are aware of the specific needs of the community should assist in selecting the program.
- Community boards and task forces should select program components that will harmonize with the political and cultural values of the community.
- The program should provide a full range of activities and services, including structured and unstructured play, rest, meals, and other fun and enrichment activities.

Identifying, Recruiting, and Retaining High-Risk Families

The need for early childhood education programs is greatest for children in high-risk families, and some evidence suggests that these programs' effects are greatest for such children. Yet high-risk families are least likely to seek out early childhood education programs. Kindergarten is not compulsory in many states, and so many high-risk children do not even have that benefit. But before high-risk parents can be approached and involved, they must be identified. Ways to accomplish this include:

- Searching local birth records for mothers who were below the age of twenty-one at the time of birth and whose children would now be two to five years old
- Seeking referrals from public health nurses, physicians, or hospitals
- Seeking referrals from local welfare services
- Using the media to recruit parents (see Chapter Twelve)

Once parents have been identified, perhaps the most appropriate and straightforward approach is to visit mothers (and fathers, if present) at home. The main purpose of this visit is to explain the services available and the benefits for the child. Visits should be made by skilled people who have experience working with families and are sensitive to the needs and culture of the community.

Involving and retaining parents in an early childhood education program can be the biggest challenge. It is more likely that parents will continue to participate in parent training if the program helps them overcome obvious obstacles to attendance such as baby-sitting and transportation. It helps if the parents receive support from their own families and friends in their participation, so find a way to involve social support networks in encouraging parents to participate. The training provided by the program must also be relevant to parents' needs. In some cases, this may mean helping parents address basic survival needs such as finding jobs or housing.

A program that requires parents to attend meetings at a central location and provides little or no support is likely to be less effective than a design incorporating home visits. A good design for the parent training component is to combine parenting training with frequent (weekly or biweekly) home visits and small-group sessions for parents located in the community. The small-group sessions should be led by a trained community outreach worker and focus on the content of the parent training. Putting parents in touch with needed resources in the community can be an important part of these meetings. Group discussions and home visits should support parents in resolving child-rearing, family, education, or work-life problems identified by the parents themselves.

Training and Technical Assistance

Training and technical assistance for early childhood education can be sought from local experts. Local early childhood education specialists can be found through universities, colleges, and community colleges. Two sources of information about early childhood education programs, training, and credentials are the National Association for the Education of Young Children, with a national network of more than 70,000 early childhood professionals in 380 affiliated groups, and the national network of Headstart Preschool programs. Head Start programs serve both rural and urban areas in all fifty states, the District of Columbia, and the Trust Territories. There are special programs for Native American and migrant children. In addition, Head Start funds thirty-eight Parent and Child Centers across the country, providing services for children age zero to three.

Evaluation

Process Evaluation

Strength and fidelity of implementation—that is, whether the program model is being used correctly—is the emphasis of process evaluation for this program element. The extent to which the target population is actually reached is also important. Other issues to consider include the quantity and quality of program services. Process areas to assess include the following:

- The number of hours of contact high-risk children and their parents have with the program or center
- The number of home visits
- The number of high-risk children and parents involved and the number and types of parent meetings held and parents attending them
- The content of actual lessons
- The content of interactions between home visitors and parents

Outcome Evaluation

Short-term effectiveness should be evaluated based on individual student outcomes and family outcomes. Short-term outcomes to assess include the following:
- Improvements in children's conduct problems
- Increases in children's language skills
- Increased clarity and consistency of discipline practices among teachers and parents
- Increased child self-management skills
- Increased family bonding

Because the "fade-out" effect is so persistent in many early childhood education programs, evaluations ideally will follow participating children and control groups throughout their school careers to examine academic progress, commitment to school, and problem behaviors. It is important to ensure that short-term benefits of the program do not disappear.

Resources

For further information, contact:
  National Association for the Education of Young Children
  1834 Connecticut Avenue, N.W.
  Washington, DC 20009-5786
  (800) 424-2460

  Project Head Start
  Administration for Children, Youth, and Families
  Office of Human Development Services
  Department of Health and Human Services
  P.O. Box 1182
  Washington, DC 20013

. . . or your Regional Office of the U.S. Department of Health and Human Services.

Chapter 7

Parent Training

Overview

Parent training programs teach skills to help parents counter risk factors and promote the key protective factors of effective family management and bonding. Many parent training programs are available for communities, fewer are well established as effective in targeting particular risk factors in particular populations. This chapter contains general guidelines for considering parent training programs to reduce risk and strengthen protective factors against adolescent substance abuse and describes three different but complementary programs for parents of children of different ages and stages of development. All are designed for groups of approximately ten to twenty-five parents.

- The *Parents and Children Videotape Series,* for parents of children aged three to ten, focuses on behavior management and problem solving.
- *How to Help Your Child Succeed in School* provides parents with

ways to improve their children's academic performance and adjustment to school.

- *Preparing for the Drug (Free) Years,* for parents of children in grades four through eight, guides families in developing a clear position on drug use that all family members will support, strengthens family bonding, and empowers family members to resist social influences to use drugs.

Parenting education should begin prenatally and continue through the years of parental responsibility. The parenting education approaches described in this chapter are for parents of children aged approximately three to thirteen years.

Problems/risk factors addressed in this chapter are poor family management practices, early antisocial behavior, academic failure, parental drug use and favorable attitudes toward use, friends who use drugs, and early first use of drugs.

Protective factors addressed in this chapter are bonding to family, skills for positive communication within the family, commitment to school, skills to interact with school personnel, developmentally appropriate opportunities for involvement in the family, clear norms against alcohol and other drug use, and skills to resist antisocial influences.

Setting the Stage

Parents are a key factor, often *the* key factor, in a child's development. The focus of parent training programs, like that of early childhood education, is on *primary prevention* — providing parents with effective ways to handle their families, support their children's academic progress, and prevent drug use and related problems later on. Parent training can also be an effective strategy for families with youngsters who have already begun using drugs or alcohol.

This chapter describes three programs that educate groups of ten to twenty-five parents in ways to reduce their children's risk of drug abuse. Each of the programs offered for this element consists of a clearly defined training program for parents with a specific curriculum and related materials. All three programs share common goals, yet each has unique characteristics associated with its focus on a specific period of child development and specific risk factors. An important theme throughout, one that needs to be present in any parent training program, is the emphasis on providing parents with skills and methods to counter risk factors faced by their children and to promote more effective family management and bonding. Community boards choosing this element may want to use a combination of one or more of these and other existing programs in the community. That choice will depend largely on the community's assessment of risks and existing programs and resources. The community's goal should be to have a developmentally complete series of parent training opportunities available for families with children ranging from birth through adolescence—opportunities that are specifically aimed at family-related risk factors for drug and alcohol abuse.

Rationale

Programs that help parents develop family management skills and provide support at home for their children's education are considered increasingly important today. There are two main reasons for the current emphasis on parent involvement. First, parents are a major influence in the development of their children, whether or not they make conscious efforts to be effective parents. In the last two decades, research has consistently shown that parents and the family can either contribute to risk or reduce it. Many of the risk factors for drug abuse are directly family-related, including poor family management practices, a family history of alcoholism, and permissive parental attitudes toward drug use. Family bonding is a key protective factor that can be strengthened by improving family communication and family management practices. Because parenting is so fundamental to child development, interventions directed toward parents have also been found to reduce other risk factors related to drug abuse, such as early aggressive behavior, poor school adjustment, and delinquent behavior (Hawkins et al., 1992).

The second reason for emphasizing parent training is related to the changing structure of American families. Every year, approximately one million children are involved in a divorce. Some 60 percent of American children spend part of their childhood in single-parent families. Constraints on time can seriously inhibit single parents' ability to be involved in their children's lives. Poverty and work schedules make it difficult for single parents to supervise and support their children. In two-parent families as well, economic pressures and desire for personal fulfillment have pushed both mothers and fathers into full-time employment. The problems associated with changing family structures, employment patterns, and poverty have far-reaching effects. The ways in which parents structure the family environment in the face of these problems and how they monitor, reinforce, reward, or punish their children's behavior are important factors in reducing risks for drug use and related problems (Fraser, Hawkins, & Howard, 1988).

Because of changes in the ways families are organized today, a parent training program should provide parents and other adult caregivers with risk reduction information and skills applicable to the myriad settings in which children live and develop. Programs may be offered through schools, community service centers, work settings, health maintenance organizations, hospitals, public health clinics, or other social service agencies. The skills taught in parent training will benefit day-care providers, grandparents, foster parents, and school personnel as they are asked to supplement or fill in for overwhelmed or absent parents. Basic criteria for assessing parent training from a preventive perspective are listed in Exhibit 7.1.

Goals and Objectives

Goals

- To alter or counteract poor family management practices, early antisocial behavior, academic failure, parental drug use and favorable attitudes toward use, friends who use drugs, and early first use of drugs
- To promote bonding to family, skills for positive communication within the family, commitment to school, clear norms against alcohol and other drug use, and skills to resist antisocial influences

Objectives

1. The *Parents and Children Videotape Series* teaches parents how to:
    *   Set clear expectations for their children's behavior
    *   Monitor their children's behavior
    *   Reinforce positive behavior in their children
    *   Provide consequences for inappropriate behavior
    *   Develop and use effective communication skills
    *   Use basic problem-solving skills for child management
2. *How to Help Your Child Succeed in School* teaches parents how to:
    *   Set up a positive learning environment in the home
    *   Become the child's at-home teacher, assisting with basic reading and math skills
    *   Interact with the child's teachers to support learning
    *   Support the completion of schoolwork at home to promote the child's school achievement
3. *Preparing for the Drug (Free) Years* seeks to:
    *   Provide parents with information about drug use and risk factors so they can be better prepared to work on preventing drug use by family members
    *   Empower parents to set a clear family position on drug use by family members
    *   Provide parents and children with the skills to refuse offers to use drugs
    *   Increase family bonding both by reducing conflict and by increasing children's involvement in positive family activities

**Exhibit 7.1. Criteria for Effective
Prevention-Oriented Parent Training.**

An effective program will

> offer training before children exhibit serious problem behavior
> address risk factors that can be changed by family action
> empower parents to decide how to apply the program in their own homes
> be culturally sensitive
> use skills training methods
> strengthen family bonds
> create a parent support network

Supporting Research

Parent training programs have been linked with a variety of positive family and child outcomes, ranging from improved family interaction to reduced child problem behaviors and improved school adjustment. Extensive research has demonstrated that when parents are taught skills to improve family management practices, to clarify and create consistency in rewards and punishments for behavior, and to promote family bonding, the result can be long-term gains for children. Parent training of the kind represented in this component has been found to be more effective than other approaches in reducing delinquency and problem behavior (Fraser et al., 1988; McMahon & Forehand, 1984; Patterson, Chamberlain, & Reid, 1982). These outcomes have been observed for children from socioeconomically disadvantaged families and for children who have exhibited early conduct disorders (Hawkins et al., 1992). The programs selected for inclusion in this chapter are examples of parent training programs with promise for reducing risk factors for adolescent drug and alcohol abuse. Each is bolstered by evidence of success in reducing specific risk factors. Taken together, they provide the kind of comprehensive, developmentally complete parent training system that is necessary for effective risk reduction across childhood and early adolescence.

The *Parents and Children Videotape Series,* developed by Carolyn Webster-Stratton of the University of Washington, has been extensively researched and field-tested with families of both well-adjusted children and children with conduct problems. It is based on the premise that people change as a result of their daily interactions with one another. Consequently, when children misbehave and families become disrupted, it is necessary to alter both the parents' behavior and the child's. Parents who took this course were able to reduce their children's behavior problems significantly and to increase positive social behaviors (Webster-Stratton, Kolpacoff, & Hollinsworth, 1989). They reported feeling more comfortable about their parenting skills after completing the course, and similar effects were found in follow-up studies (Webster-Stratton, 1982, 1989; Webster-Stratton, Kolpacoff,

& Hollinsworth, 1988). Another study of the program found that its use of interactive videotapes reduced the time required of trainer/therapists. Even when the videotapes were used alone for self-instruction, they were effective (Webster-Stratton, 1984).

How to Help Your Child Succeed in School, a program developed by the authors of this book, is offered to parents at a critical time in their children's social and academic development— just as the child is entering and adjusting to elementary school. Studies have shown that children's attitudes toward education are shaped by their parent's attitudes and that student achievement increases when parents are actively involved in supporting their children's learning. But research has also revealed that most parents do not know what is expected of their children in the classroom. Across the socioeconomic spectrum, parents universally view a good education as key to their children's success. However, academic success is something not all families have experienced or know how to promote. This program teaches parents how to provide important help and support for learning at home. When used as part of a comprehensive intervention with teachers and parents, *How to Help Your Child Succeed in School* was associated with better parenting skills and lower rates of child aggressiveness (Hawkins, Von Cleve, & Catalano, 1991). It was positively correlated with parent reports of frequency of their interaction with teachers, educational expectations for their child, time spent reading with the child, and perceived consistency in the perceptions of parents and teachers (Hawkins, Catalano, Jones, & Fine, 1987).

The support offered at home for a child's work at school can be an important factor in the child's academic success. If the television set is always on at home, if there is no quiet place for the child to do schoolwork, and if the parent offers no encouragement or opportunity for schoolwork to be done, this communicates that schoolwork is relatively unimportant. In contrast, parents who provide opportunities for children to develop academic skills at home, who are in contact with their child's teacher, and who reinforce school achievement and completion of homework can help their children to avoid school adjustment problems and contribute to their children's academic success.

Preparing for the Drug (Free) Years, developed by the authors of this book, includes a specific focus on the prevention of alcohol and other drug use in training for effective family management as children enter adolescence. It provides ways for parents to define and communicate a family position on drug use, involving their children in its development. The program also provides an opportunity for parents and children together to learn and practice refusal skills and skills to manage family conflict. The program helps parents restructure roles and expectations for family participation as their children enter a new stage of development.

Preparing for the Drug (Free) Years has been implemented widely in metropolitan and statewide campaigns involving thousands of parents and volunteer workshop leaders. Research shows that when the program is implemented in this way, parents acquire skills, attitudes, and parenting practices that are associated with lower drug use risks in children (Hawkins, Catalano, & Kent, 1991).

Program Description

The Parents and Children Videotape Series

The series consists of two phases. In the first, the emphasis is on positive interaction between parents and children — playing together, planning enjoyable activities together, and so on. The second phase emphasizes monitoring, limit setting, and problem solving. Parents learn to develop a consistent reward structure for appropriate, compliant behavior in children, and to use consistent and moderate punishment when children do not behave appropriately. The program emphasizes communication skills and ways to manage anger, which helps increase positive interaction and bonding in the family.

The program consists of ten facilitator-led sessions for groups of ten to twenty parents. Participants see videotaped vignettes of common family situations, such as a parent having difficulty getting a child to do a task, or a child coming home from school and not getting attention from the parent. The workshop leader facilitates a discussion of what could be done in each situation, and then the parents see both "good" and "bad" solutions to problems on videotape. Each session begins with a discussion of the homework assignment from the previous week, then new material is presented through the videotaped vignettes. A detailed workshop leader's guide is provided, but the structure of the sessions is flexible. Manuals and workbooks guide participants through the series of program topics, which include the following:

- How to Play with a Child
- Helping Children Learn
- The Art of Effective Praising
- Tangible Rewards
- How to Set Limits
- Helping Children Learn to Accept Limits
- Dealing with Noncompliance
- Avoiding and Ignoring Misbehavior
- Time Out and Other Penalties
- Preventive Approaches

The following comments from a workshop illustrate what parents of children with conduct disorders have learned from the *Parents and Children Videotape Series*.

Mother: By keeping track of praises I was able to be aware of all the positive things he does. It is so easy to get bent up and think, "he can't do anything right." All of a sudden you start listening to yourself saying, "You did a nice job there. Thank you!" Once I started to be specific in my praises, I noticed how many areas he is really trying to do right. You start thinking, "he's capable. He's probably been doing this a lot longer than I was willing to listen or give him credit for."

Father: . . . through bad habits and exhaustion I was using too much power. So I backed off and we don't have the power struggles any more.

Mother: . . . now when I interact with her I tend to look at her eyes and I realize I can't remember my parents ever doing that. I'm giving her more space and time. . . . I'm trying to give her more independence, when she wants to do something let her do it, rather than saying, "you're going to spill the milk all over the floor."

Father: You know, [children] should be treated as equal human beings — it doesn't mean you don't set limits and all that stuff, but it means you know that they're human beings and as deserving of respect as you are. (Spitzer, Webster-Stratton, & Hollinsworth, 1991, pp. 419, 424)

How to Help Your Child Succeed in School

This program for groups of ten to twenty-five parents consists of five two-hour sessions delivered by a team of two leaders. The program is structured so that during the first session, participants select from a menu of specific topics those most relevant to their own family needs. Resource materials to help parents understand what their children are being taught in school are obtained through the local school or school district where the workshops are offered. The program teaches parents to reinforce at home what the child is learning at school and develop consistency between home and school. To achieve these goals, parents learn how to interact more effectively with their child's teacher, and how to encourage the child's skill development at home.

Skill-building games that parents and children can play together supplement and strengthen the child's learning. During the last twenty minutes of each session, parents learn and practice with their children activities that they can continue to use at home. A parent workbook with homework assignments for the parents to carry out with their children between sessions and a detailed workshop leader's guide are included in the program. Participants select from the following topics:

- Establishing a positive home environment for learning
- Strengthening children's reading skills

- Using language arts games
- Strengthening children's math skills
- Helping with homework
- Home-school communications
- What to do about television
- Being an effective parent teacher

Preparing for the Drug (Free) Years

Facilitated by two co-leaders, at least one of whom is a parent, this program consists of five two-hour sessions for groups of approximately twenty parents. Interactive videotapes portray family situations that illustrate the parenting issues for each session's topic, serving as starting points for group discussion. The videotapes model skills for setting family rules, refusal skills, effective family management techniques, conflict management skills, and skills to promote positive bonding within the family. Participants practice these skills in small groups before using them at home with their children. Each participant receives a family activity book with worksheets and homework assignments to complete between the sessions. A detailed workshop leader's guide is provided. Sessions follow a similar format, as follows:

- Introductory exercises to foster development of a parent network supporting values antithetical to drug use among children.
- A combination of live presentations by workshop leaders and video instruction.
- Exercises designed to build skills.
- Assignment: hold a family meeting to practice the skills and discuss the topic taught in that session. (In the following session, parents report on the assignment.)

The topics for the five sessions are the following:

- Getting Started: How to Prevent Drug Abuse in Your Family
- How to Develop a Family Position on Drugs

- Avoiding Trouble: How to Say No to Drugs
- Managing Conflict: How to Express and Control Your Anger
- Involving Everyone: How to Strengthen Family Bonds

The following comments, taken from evaluation forms completed by leaders and participants following sessions, provide a sampling of parents' responses to *Preparing for the Drug (Free) Years:*

> One parent who recently attended a PDFY workshop told the leader he had "never clarified in his own mind exactly what he thought about his children's use of drugs" before the training.
> —Kent, Washington PDFY training workshop

> Our parents shared the realization that they needed to reach agreement between themselves over what behaviors are appropriate before they could reach agreement with their children about a family drug policy.
> —Kent, Washington PDFY training workshop

> The vehicles for family communication — the family meeting and parents' ability to retain and continue using family conflict skills — offer long-term benefits in our community.
> —PDFY trainer, Vancouver, Washington

> A divorced mother attended a PDFY training workshop at her child's junior high school. The first session made her aware of the scope and extent of her own drinking problem. As a result, she entered therapy to bring her own life under control before her problems harmed her child further.
> —Notes from a Chicago-area PDFY training workshop

Implementation

Community groups that have identified family risk factors as a priority focus through a risk and resource assessment of the community should establish a parent training task force. This task force will select which new parent training programs to implement or decide which existing parenting programs to expand in the community. The task force should recruit people from the community to lead the training sessions and arrange for training of these leaders in the programs selected. Program developers can provide training, materials, and technical assistance to communities for successful implementation of their programs. The task force will oversee implementation, including identification of workshop sites, recruitment of parents, and management of the logistics and arrangements.

Organization

The task force should work in partnership with agencies and organizations that can help to support parent training, such as local schools, the PTA, volunteer organizations, service clubs, businesses, religious organizations, and the communications media.

Workshops are best offered in sequence, rather than all at once. It would be appropriate, for example, to launch the *How to Help Your Child Succeed in School* series at the beginning of the school year. *Preparing for the Drug (Free) Years* might then be offered in the spring or in conjunction with other drug abuse prevention activities and events in the community. Ideally, components for families with children of all ages will be offered throughout the community in diverse settings and with a varied, repeated schedule to encourage participation.

The selection of workshop leaders is important to the success of these programs in the community. Leaders do not necessarily have to be professionals with advanced credentials. However, they should have had experience leading groups of adults and possess good communication skills. Leaders may be parents with leadership experience, teachers, family-life educators, nurses, physicians, social workers, or others.

Recruitment

A balance of high-risk and lower-risk families should be encouraged, although the emphasis will be on recruiting parents of high-risk children. One goal of organizing this element will be to create strong acceptance in the community for parent training as a preventive approach, to publicize the concept widely, and to involve growing numbers of parents through word of mouth. Parent training may be chosen as the theme of one of the community's media campaigns (Hawkins, Catalano, & Kent, 1991) (see Chapter Twelve). Announcements can be made at schools, through PTAs and other parent organizations, at childcare centers, in parents' work settings, and through direct recruitment of parents by teachers, principals, and other parents.

Some special effort may be needed to recruit and retain parents of children exposed to multiple risk factors, who are subject to many life stresses and who may find attendance at parent training workshops burdensome. Here are some ideas:

- Financial incentives sponsored by local businesses
- Provision for child care, including creative approaches such as videos and games so that children who attend with their parents enjoy coming and want to come again
- Provision of transportation
- Ice cream parties and socials for classrooms with the highest rates of parent attendance
- Involving teachers in contacting targeted family members to encourage them to attend
- Raffles of donated goods that require parents to attend the workshops in order to win
- Children's poster contests that require parental attendance in order for the child to win
- Culturally sensitive leadership
- An attractive, easily accessible setting

Characteristics of the recruiters will also affect the participation of high-risk parents. It is important to involve people in the community who are trusted and respected — for example, local clergy, other parents, community role models, and representatives of the local communications media. According to a trainer for *Preparing for the Drug (Free) Years* in Vancouver, Washington, "We've had the most success when we've had volunteers at the school who have been through the program and are outgoing in nature. Having gone through the program, they're very committed, and being outgoing, they're comfortable standing up and talking about this program. When we have this kind of help, we have always filled each workshop."

If the program is useful and relevant to the parents, attendance will not be a problem. All three of the programs included here, like other successful parenting training programs, have received high ratings from parents; once recruited, parents are likely to want to continue attending the sessions.

Site Selection and Sponsorship

Different types of sites are appropriate for different communities. Sites should be provided by organizations and agencies that support parent training in cooperation with the community board. Careful site selection is especially important in high-risk communities where safety, transportation, and institutional intimidation can be barriers. Churches or meeting rooms in housing projects and community centers are among the possible sites for these communities. The same workshop might be offered in several different settings at the same time to reach a variety of parents.

Training and Technical Assistance

Workshop leaders should have experience in group leadership and adult education. Training teaches effective means for delivering each specific program. A two- to four-day training program for the *Parents and Children Videotape Series* is offered twice a year. Three days of training are required for leaders of *How to Help Your Child Succeed in School* and *Preparing for the Drug (Free) Years.* Contact the resources at the end of the chapter for information on training schedules and technical assistance in planning and implementing these parent training programs.

Evaluation

Process Evaluation

Training for workshop leaders should be evaluated through written assessments of the participants' skills, knowledge, attitudes, and satisfaction with the training. Similar procedures should be included for each of the parent training sessions. Pretests and posttests should measure baseline and postprogram knowledge and skills, and follow-up measures should determine how often parents actually use the techniques they have learned. Acceptability measures should assess the extent to which parents find the specific techniques useful and comfortable to use at home.

Outcome Evaluation

Evaluation of the overall effects of parent training should include follow-up studies of the families involved in each component to assess parents' and children's behavior and interaction patterns at appropriate intervals after the parents have completed the program. Specific outcome indicators should be linked to the specific program objectives, and, depending on the program implemented, will include evidence of clear parental expectations for child behavior, use of problem-solving and communication skills, use of behavior reinforcement mechanisms, increased (positive) parent-teacher interaction, home learning environment supportive of schoolwork, use of family interaction skills, reduction of conflict, and increased positive family activities. Videotaped observations of parent-child interaction and home visits for data gathering are strategies to employ where feasible. Measures may also include self-reporting forms filled out by the children of participating parents and telephone interviews with parents. Specific program evaluation materials are available from the program developers listed below.

Resources

For training and technical assistance information and materials on the *Parents and Children Videotape Series,* contact:

Carolyn Webster-Stratton, Ph.D.
Family and Child Guidance
1411-8th Avenue West
Seattle, WA 98119

For training and technical assistance information and materials on *How to Help Your Child Succeed in School* and *Preparing for the Drug (Free) Years,* contact:
Developmental Research and Programs, Inc.
130 Nickerson Street, Suite 107
Seattle, WA 98109
Phone: (800) 736-2630

Chapter 8

School Organization
and Management

Overview

This program element focuses on two approaches that have
helped schools to become significantly more protective as environments for child development and bonding. They reflect
a widespread concern that schools have not provided adequate
support to children at risk and those who teach them. Special
supplementary programs, pull-out classes (those that remove
children from their normal classroom setting), and even changes
in the curriculum ignore basic structural and systemic issues:
how schools are organized, how they are governed, and how
administrators and teachers interact with parents, students, and
the community. The *School Development Program,* created by James
Comer and colleagues at the Yale Child Study Center, is an
organizational development model focusing on broadening the
involvement of those who have a stake in a particular school.
It creates a school management team, a mental health team,
and a program to encourage and support parent involvement

at the building level. The *Program Development Evaluation (PDE)* method, developed by G. D. Gottfredson and D. C. Gottfredson at the Center for Social Organization of Schools at Johns Hopkins University, is an organizational development model that can be applied to individual schools or to an entire school district. It offers schools a system for assessment, analysis, and action to solve school problems.

The *School Development Program* has been used in elementary schools, middle schools, and schools that combine grades K-8. The *Program Development Evaluation* method has been used at all grade levels as well as for districtwide reorganization.

Problems/risk factors addressed in this chapter are antisocial behavior, academic failure, alienation, rebelliousness, association with drug-using peers, community disorganization, transitions, and mobility.

Protective factors addressed in this chapter are bonding to school, family, and neighborhood; opportunities for involvement among school personnel and parents; recognition for positive behavior, activities, and accomplishments; and skills for effective interaction of school personnel and parents.

Setting the Stage

Teaching and learning cannot be significantly improved until the underlying development and management issues in a school are addressed [Comer, 1988, p. 46].

Today, children come to school from family circumstances dramatically different from those of a generation ago — the emergence of children living with no biological parent, a growing number of single-parent families, a majority of two-parent families with both parents working outside the home, increasing numbers of children in poverty, and diminished support systems in the community. The changes in the world outside the schools present the educational system with unprecedented challenges. This chapter describes two promising approaches for improving the organization and management of schools to cope more effectively with these changes.

The School Development Program has gained recognition for improving students' behavior and academic performance in a variety of communities. The program creates three major support systems at the school: a governance and management team, a mental health team, and a parent program. Parents, teachers, and administrators play active and meaningful roles in all these groups, resulting in a greatly enhanced sense of "ownership" of the school's programs and bonding to the school. Instead of the intimidating presence many parents of children at risk have perceived their children's schools to be, the schools now welcome and support parents with a positive educational climate for everyone. The program can be particularly beneficial where school-community relationships have been characterized by distrust or poor communication.

The Program Development Evaluation (PDE) method provides a mechanism for assessment, analysis, and action to solve school problems that can significantly enhance school climate and management.

Rationale

A movement to examine closely the management practices of schools is currently gaining support among educators and policy makers throughout the country. This movement has been stimulated by reports on the poor quality of American education, notably the 1983 publication of *A Nation at Risk* by the National Commission on Excellence in Education, and more recently by the establishment of six National Education Goals for the Year 2000 by the National Education Goals Panel.

Most of the reforms have sought to make schools more demanding and rigorous, centering on such issues as longer school days, more demanding curricula, more homework, and higher standards for graduation and grade-level advancement. Such reforms have taken hold throughout the country, stimulated both by state legislation and by formulation of the six National Educational Goals. They are likely to influence schools for the foreseeable future. These are worthwhile goals, for American schools have been lax in challenging students and in providing them with the academic skills they will need to manage the information and technologies of the future. However, educators and policy makers have increasingly recognized that focusing exclusively on standardized test scores and knowledge outcomes overlooks important needs among students who come to school poorly prepared for learning.

The Carnegie Council on Adolescent Development, in its landmark report *Turning Points* (1989), pointed directly to school structure as a major problem at the middle school level. Many of the same comments also apply to high schools and, especially in high-risk communities, elementary schools. This report expressed the concern that many young people fall behind, and their intellectual and emotional needs go unmet, in the large middle schools that "process" them. Among other recommendations, the Carnegie report emphasized smaller, more personal school units (subschools or "family groupings"); more meaningful contact between children and caring adults; an emphasis on success for all students; and closer, more trusting relationships between the school, students, and parents, leading to "a community of shared purpose."

These recommendations are consistent with the social development strategy that undergirds "Communities That Care." Students are more likely to experience personal success when they have the skills and opportunities to perform challenging and meaningful tasks and when they receive recognition for completing such tasks. In turn, they will be more bonded to the social units that offer skills, opportunities, and rewards. These are the kinds of reforms being called for by educational leaders who focus on school organization and management practices.

An organizational development approach to school reform emphasizes basic organizational changes. This approach is consistent with the findings of researchers who have examined the impact of the school's organizational climate on student learning and school effectiveness (Brookover et al., 1982; Goodlad, 1984). Organizational development offers a way to address students' social, emotional, and learning problems holistically, emphasizing children's interaction with the social and cultural environment they inhabit at home and at school.

The developers of the school management approaches

described here look beyond the content of the curriculum or special programs for children with problems and ask one basic question: How is the school's organization contributing to its problems, and how can these organizational structures be changed?

Goals and Objectives

Goals
- To alter or counteract antisocial behavior, academic failure, alienation, rebelliousness, association with drug-using peers, community disorganization, and transitions and mobility
- To promote bonding to school, family, and neighborhood; opportunities for involvement of school personnel and parents; recognition for positive behavior, activities, and accomplishments; and skills for effective interaction of school personnel and parents

Objectives
- To make schools more productive, positive places in which all young people have the best possible opportunities, support, and recognition for success
- To provide schools with specific structures for creating a sense of unity, coherence, trust, shared power and decision making, and mutual support in dealing with the problems of children and families
- To involve parents in their children's education by creating a closer school-parent-community relationship and encouraging parents to be active participants in the educational process
- To teach administrators and teachers a well-defined and tested method for assessing and resolving school-related problems and implementing change

Supporting Research

A wide body of research supports effective school management as a way to promote bonding and improved academic achievement, particularly among low-income and minority students

(Brookover et al., 1982). Parent involvement, a main feature of the School Development Program, has been identified as a particularly important factor (Chubb, 1988).

The School Development Program was first applied to inner-city schools in New Haven, Connecticut, beginning in 1968. When the program was initiated, the two elementary schools that were to receive the program ranked near the bottom of the city's schools in reading and mathematics scores. After more than a decade of this program, without any change in the socioeconomic makeup of the student population, fourth-grade students in the first school ranked third among all New Haven schools in academic achievement, and those in the second school ranked fourth. A follow-up study of children who participated in the School Development Program found that they scored higher than a matched comparison group in reading and math, school grades earned, and social competency (Cauce, Comer, & Schwartz, 1987; Comer, 1988). The two schools have also experienced higher attendance rates and fewer discipline problems since program implementation. The School Development Program is now being used in more than 100 schools throughout the country, including the school systems of Prince Georges County, Maryland; Benton Harbor, Michigan; and Norfolk, Virginia.

The PDE method has been studied and implemented in the school districts of Baltimore, Maryland, and Charleston, South Carolina. It has also been used in Compton and Pasadena, California; Chicago; Kalamazoo, Michigan; and New York City. A 1988 report on the Baltimore program found dramatic improvements in the participating schools, including significant increases in teacher morale and innovation and decreases in rebellious behavior and negative student attitudes toward school. A 1989 evaluation of PDE in six Charleston schools found that, in comparison with control schools, those using the PDE method improved significantly in several measures of program effectiveness, including classroom order, classroom organization, and clarity of rules. Some schools reported greater improvement than others, and strong leadership by the school improvement team was found to be a key factor in their success (D. C. Gottfredson, Karweit, & G. D. Gottfredson, 1989).

Program Description

The School Development Program

Three main components form this program: the governance and management team, the mental health team, and a parent program.

The governance and management team is made up of the school principal, two teachers selected by the faculty, three parents selected by the school's parent group, and a mental health professional. This group meets every week. Charged with the main responsibility for school-site planning and program development, the group considers such issues as the following:

- Schoolwide needs and goals
- Curriculum
- Inservice training
- School climate
- Program implementation
- Resources
- Evaluation

The governance and management team also works closely with the other groups established by the program to plan and carry out schoolwide activities over the course of the year.

The mental health team includes a classroom teacher, the special education teacher, a social worker, and a school psychologist. They, too, meet weekly, to consider individual student behavior problems. The team diversity helps to ensure that problems and solutions are considered from several vantage points. Through its delegate on the governance and management team, the mental health team also recommends and helps to bring about changes in school policies and procedures that affect the school's social climate and its students' well-being. Developing an orientation program for new students and their parents to introduce them to the school is one example. The team approach facilitates identification of patterns of behavioral problems and determination of whether the school is contributing to these problems in any way (Comer, 1988).

Parents have many opportunities to become involved in addition to their representation on the governance and management team. They are drawn into the school through social activities, workshops, and opportunities to serve as classroom tutors or aides. The program provides a parent handbook describing parental roles and opportunities for involvement. The following example illustrates the benefits of parent involvement:

> At a school in Maryland, the school planning and management team became aware of a decline in the students' math scores. Parents on the team requested a workshop that would teach them methods they could use at home to improve their children's math skills. A subcommittee decided on the specific methods and organized a workshop led jointly by parents and teachers. Then the methods were used by parents at home and reinforced by teachers at school.

A set of key assumptions governs all facets of the School Development Program:

- The principal is recognized as the school's leader and main authority. Still, the relationship between the principal, the faculty, the parents, and the students is one of mutual respect and reciprocity.
- Decision making is shared and participatory. Whenever possible, decisions are made by consensus.
- The focus is on problem solving, not blaming.

According to Comer (1988, p. 45),

> Schools implementing the *School Development Program* are characterized by an atmosphere of informality and enthusiasm. There is an attitude of mutual respect among administrators, teachers and other staff members, students, and parents. Parents are visible at the school in a variety of roles — as mem-

bers of the Governance and Management Team or the Mental Health Team, working as aides or tutors in classrooms, and helping to sponsor and carry out social events. The school might have a "Discovery Room" for children who have lost interest in learning — instead of labeling them as "problems." Potluck dinners, book fairs, and other events regularly bring parents, students, and teachers together in a positive way. Children who are having difficulty receive individual help and attention through the Mental Health Team. The entire school climate is conducive to orderliness, cooperation, collaboration, and learning.

The Program Development Evaluation Method

The PDE method revolves around a careful and systematic assessment of school problems. This assessment is used as the basis for a plan to tighten management by creating explicit standards for performance, communicating those standards throughout the school, assessing implementation of programs in accordance with the standards, and adjusting the plan when needed. The process involves a set of specific steps (G. D. Gottfredson & D. C. Gottfredson, 1989, p. 12):

- Use assessment information to define problems and translate those problems into concrete, measurable goals.
- Determine factors that are causing problems and choose potential interventions that address those factors.
- Select proven or promising interventions to bring about the desired outcomes.
- Use information about the factors working both for and against the innovation as part of the planning for program implementation.
- Specify critical benchmarks, implementation standards, and time-delineated tasks to serve as indicators of progress.
- Monitor all aspects of program implementation and outcomes to signal needed changes in course.

- Accept that program development occurs over time, that emergent problems will require resolution, and that program refinement rather than abandonment is necessary for organizational effectiveness.

These steps are carried out by a school improvement team of teachers, parents, school administrators, and district-level staff. The team meets regularly to identify priorities, clarify goals and objectives, develop programs that address problem areas, and monitor the process of implementing programs. The method provides for continuing scrutiny of changes in outcomes associated with changes in school management.

Implementation

Implementation of school organization and management programs requires a careful process of establishing school district commitment to the program and selecting participating schools through an assessment of readiness as illustrated in Exhibit 8.1. If, through a process of risk and resource assessment, a community board identifies school risk factors that require action, a task force for school organization should be established. It should be formed of specific members from the target schools, the central district, and the community. In replicating the school development program in Benton Harbor, Michigan, for example, Comer and his associates (phone interview with staff of Social Development Research Group) used the following steps:

- Selection of a change agent — an administrator to coordinate and direct implementation of the program in the school district
- Intensive training of the school district's representative through on-site observation at the Yale Child Study Center
- A full year for district planning to begin implementation of the program
- Establishment of a subcommittee to oversee implementation of the program

Exhibit 8.1. Questions to Determine
a School's Readiness for Change.

- Is the school free of a history of failed efforts at implementing programs?
- Is a clear problem openly identified?
- Is morale high? Is there cooperation and support among people in the school?
- Can the school openly anticipate obstacles and develop strategies to cope with them?
- Does the principal foster upward communication of both good and bad news?
- Is there any indication that teams of faculty members have worked together to accomplish anything of note in the recent past?
- Is there pressure from the community, school system, or other outside source for change?
- Do faculty and administrators talk of problems of potentially manageable scale (or do they define problems as too large to tackle)?
- Do administrators and faculty speak of factors over which the school has control in discussing problems? (Or do they blame sources beyond the school's control such as family poverty, discrimination in society in general for problems?)

If the answers to most of these questions are "yes," then your school probably has the capacity to launch an ambitious program. If the answer to one or more questions is "no," then ask how your program planning can help turn the answer to "yes."

—from G. D. Gottfredson (1988, p. 16)

- School selection according to the following criteria: (1) the principal's interest in the program, (2) a low level of student achievement, and (3) a high rate of student behavior problems
- Intensive training for the school administrators — topic areas include child development in the preschool years, the relationship of child development and academic and social behavior at school, shared governance and management, social development, and development of student achievement
- A program orientation for school and community members, including presentations about the program to local business leaders
- Actual implementation of the program

Both the School Development Program and the PDE method require the full commitment of the school's principal, faculty, and parents for at least three years. It will take time to build this support. From the start, there must be strong leadership among the principal and key faculty members. The principal's own management style will be a particularly important factor in the success or failure of the program; flexibility and a collaborative approach are essential.

Resources such as special staff, release time for staff development, special scheduling, and facilities and space are also needed. To make sure this support will be available, a commitment to providing needed resources on the part of the district's governing board and superintendent will be an important factor in deciding to initiate this program element. The most effective strategy is to develop top-level support for the program first. Over time, more and more people in the schools and the community will become familiar with the program and recognize the value of investing substantial time and energy in its implementation.

Training and Technical Assistance

Training and technical assistance for these school development and management approaches are available from program developers listed in the Resources section at the end of this chapter.

The School Development Program was awarded over $5 million from the Rockefeller Foundation for national dissemination between 1990 and 1995. The program requires that a school district program coordinator be selected and trained in New Haven for three to four weeks. The training offers in-depth exposure to the program and implementation procedures. A three-day orientation is also provided for school staff and parents. Program staff follow up through on-site and telephone consultation.

With the recent establishment of the Comer Project for Change in Education (CPCE), a new dimension has been added to the training. A two-week institute, offered twice a year, provides intensive training in several important areas, including school change, child development, organizational behavior, and action research. School districts must meet specific criteria before they are accepted to receive training for implementing the School Development Program.

The PDE method also requires that the coordinator participate in a training program. The duration of the program varies, depending on the background of the coordinator, from four hours for a coordinator experienced in organizational development and research to three weeks for a person with no experience in either area. Training contracts are negotiated individually. School districts sometimes divide responsibilities for implementing the PDE method among persons with different types of experience.

Evaluation

Process Evaluation

As part of the assessment and planning procedures, process evaluation is built into the School Development Program and the PDE method. Measures include:

- Participation in management and governance teams
- Numbers of new programs initiated or implemented
- Levels of parent involvement
- Surveys designed to assess teachers' and parents' attitudes toward the school and their role in school management and the educational process

Outcome Evaluation

Measures of program effectiveness might include the following:

- School records and self-reports of grades, number of students kept back in a grade, absenteeism, tardiness, disciplinary referrals, suspensions, and expulsions of students
- Survey instruments designed to assess students' levels of bonding to school and teachers and their school behaviors, including drug use

Resources

For further information about the School Development Program, contact:

School Development Program
Child Study Center
Yale University
230 So. Frontage Road
New Haven, CT 06510-8009
Phone: (203) 785-2548

For further information about the Program Development Evaluation method, contact:

Gary D. Gottfredson
Center for Social Organization of Schools
The Johns Hopkins University
3505 N. Charles Street
Baltimore, MD 21208
Phone: (301) 516-0370

Chapter 9

Instructional Improvement in Schools

Overview

Success in a child's life is defined largely by success in school. When children experience early school failure, it can become self-perpetuating — a self-fulfilling prophecy. The instructional improvement element attempts to prevent school failure by exposing all students, including those at highest risk, to teaching strategies that improve classroom climate, interactions among students and between students and teachers, and academic achievement for all. The element includes three distinct but complementary strategies: *proactive classroom management,* which involves students in their learning through more effective use of classroom time; *effective teaching strategies,* a method for designing lesson plans to motivate students, keep them actively involved in learning, and help them to achieve; and *cooperative learning,* which encourages students to work together in groups, thereby developing a wide range of social and academic skills.

All students in kindergarten through twelfth grade can be affected by instructional improvement.

Problems/risk factors addressed in this chapter are low commitment to school, academic failure, and early antisocial behavior.

Protective factors addressed in this chapter are bonding to school and positive peers, skills to establish positive social relationships, and opportunities to actively participate in learning.

Setting the Stage

You do not have to be a professional educator to know there is tremendous diversity among students in today's schools. What happens to these children in the classroom can have a major impact on their lives. Although the following examples are fictitious, both of them could be found in almost any school today — and both are directly related to the effect of schools on high-risk children, including whether or not they will abuse drugs.

Ms. Smith's Class

The students in Ms. Smith's class enter the room before the bell, then quickly get out their class materials. Talking ceases when the bell rings. The students complete a short academic task while Ms. Smith checks roll and performs other administrative tasks. When Ms. Smith calls for students to exchange papers for checking, they do it quickly. Later, when Ms. Smith is presenting new content from the day's lesson, the students are attentive and focused on the presentation. After Ms. Smith gives an assignment, the students begin work promptly. The students and the teacher are focused on learning tasks, yet the atmosphere is pleasant and relaxed.

Ms. Jones's Class

Several of the students in Ms. Jones's class enter the room after the bell rings. A few minutes of confused milling about go by before all the students are seated and Ms. Jones takes roll. Three students leave their seats before the first class activity, further delaying the start of the activity. During class recitation, many students call out without having first been called on. Sometimes students comment rudely about other students' responses. When Ms. Jones criticizes these students, they laugh out loud. Toward the end of the activity, most of the students are no longer even paying attention to it. Instead, they talk among themselves, pass notes, or engage in other activities. Ms. Jones gives a seat-work assignment, but only a few students work on it. A high noise level continues throughout the lesson.

Whatever their ability or background, students in a class like Ms. Jones's are at higher risk for school failure and related problems than students in a class like Ms. Smith's. This program element addresses a fundamental challenge to educators: the need to involve students as active learners and motivate them to succeed academically. Instructional improvement programs are designed to help teachers learn proven methods and skills to involve their students more deeply in the learning process, conduct more orderly and effective lessons, and promote a more positive and constructive classroom atmosphere throughout the school day. To do this, the element employs three distinct but complementary educational strategies:

- *Proactive classroom management* is a technique for involving students in their learning through more effective use of classroom time.
- *Effective teaching* strategies help the teacher motivate students, establish clear objectives, and constantly monitor all students' progress through regular interaction.
- *Cooperative learning* motivates students through group work and team building — students work regularly in small groups, learning social as well as academic skills.

All of these approaches combine to help students experience academic success. When students are successful academically and bonded to school, they are less likely to become involved in drug abuse or delinquency. With success comes a more positive orientation to the future and a sense of personal competence.

Rationale

Increasingly, schools are faced with heterogeneous student populations, including large numbers of students who are poorly prepared for school. One consequence is that the schools are having great difficulty teaching a significant portion of our young people. Children who experience low academic achievement and behavior problems in the primary grades often fall into a pattern of repeated failure and acting out that teachers and parents find difficult to change.

Schools have tried two distinct approaches to help children characterized by behavior problems and low academic achievement. One is to remove them from the regular classroom and put them into special education, other remedial programs, or alternative schools. This "pull-out" approach has several drawbacks: (1) It stigmatizes the children it aims to help, often worsening the self-fulfilling prophecy of failure it had hoped to alleviate; (2) it deprives children of the opportunity to associate with high-achieving and more successful peers; and (3) it places them in a separate group with only each other as role models and peer influences (Hawkins, Doueck, & Lishner, 1988).

An alternative to pull-out programs that offers more promise of success is to make changes in classroom practices, such as improved instructional practices and classroom management. These approaches have led to greater involvement and success for all students. This approach has been shown to be particularly effective for boys from low-income families (O'Donnell, Hawkins, Catalano, Abbott, & Day, 1991). Effective classroom management practices are proactive rather than reactive — they can help to reduce behavior problems in the classroom before they occur.

One of the most important factors in student learning, recent research has shown, is the amount of time actually spent engaged in learning (Walberg, 1988). Better organized classrooms allow more time to be spent on teaching and less time on reactive discipline. When students spend more time engaged in learning, student achievement improves, and bonding—to the classroom, the teacher, other students, and the school—is enhanced.

The three approaches described in this element (proactive classroom management, interactive teaching, and cooperative learning) promote opportunities for involvement, skill development, and reinforcement, all of which are central to the social development strategy. All three help to make the classroom more productive, cooperative, and orderly. Proactive classroom management minimizes time wasted on matters unrelated to learning, and interactive teaching provides teachers with a structured planning technique to motivate and involve students in learning. Cooperative learning minimizes negative peer influences in the classroom and has been associated with achievement gains. As a result, all students are provided with ways to become more bonded to the classroom and school (Hawkins & Lam, 1987).

Goals and Objectives

Goals
- To prevent, reduce, or counteract low commitment to school, academic failure, and early antisocial behavior
- To promote bonding to school and to prosocial peers

Objectives
- To provide teachers with techniques to maintain control of their classrooms without hindering children's bonding to school
- To train teachers to use effective instructional approaches
- To promote more positive interaction among all students and between students and their teachers
- To teach students the skills to establish positive social relationships

Supporting Research

The three approaches in this element have been used extensively in a variety of school settings. In one study, students in an experimental group exposed to all three approaches for one year showed significant improvements in attitudes toward math class, attachment to school, expectations for education, lowered aggression among boys, and lowered rates of suspension and expulsion from school (Hawkins et al., 1988; Hawkins & Lam, 1987; Hawkins, Von Cleve, & Catalano, 1991).

Separate studies of each of the three strategies have also found improved learning in a variety of situations (Brophy & Good, 1986; Doyle, 1986; Slavin, 1990; Walberg, 1986). In addition to studies demonstrating its contribution to time on task, proactive classroom management is strongly supported by studies of teacher effectiveness linking high academic achievement and motivation with clear, authoritative leadership and direction on the teacher's part (Brophy & Good, 1986).

Reviews of teaching practices that lead to successful academic performance provide the basis for effective teaching strategies. The results of numerous studies of teaching practices have consistently shown that "when teachers teach more systematically, student achievement improves — frequently with gains in students' attitudes toward themselves and school" (Rosenshine, 1986, p. 69).

Cooperative learning is now widely used in schools across the country and has been found to positively influence social and academic learning and intergroup relationships among students (Aronson, Bridgeman, & Geffner, 1978; Slavin, 1990). Mastery of learning tasks, motivation, positive student attitudes toward teachers and schools, and self-concept are greater in cooperative classrooms than in competitive or individualistic ones (Johnson & Johnson, 1980; Slavin, 1979).

Program Description

Proactive Classroom Management

The central focus of the proactive classroom management strategy is providing teachers with skills to maximize the time students spend actually involved in learning and to minimize classroom disruptions (Cummings, 1983). When teachers learn how to give clear and explicit instructions for student behavior and to recognize and reward attempts to comply; when they learn how to keep minor discipline problems from interrupting the learning process, then students learn to manage their own behavior. Specific proactive management strategies include the following:

- Starting the school year with clearly defined rules and expectations for behavior
- Teaching students classroom rules and routines in structured lessons
- Using praise effectively
- Making smooth transitions between classroom activities that maximize the time spent learning
- Giving clear directions
- Using classroom control methods that maintain a positive classroom environment and maximize time on task

Example

The teacher realizes that the first thing in the morning is prime learning time. But she has to handle "administrivia" first thing in the morning. To capitalize on this valuable opportunity for learning, she teaches the students how to enter the classroom, take the lunch count and attendance themselves, put field trip forms in a box while checking their names on a class list, and go to their seats for a warm-up exercise. What might take twenty-five minutes in another classroom can be accomplished here in five minutes.

Effective Teaching Strategies

This technique enhances the teacher's ability to design lesson plans that will motivate students and to monitor their learning. The method contrasts with more traditional approaches, which often overlook the needs of high-risk students. Specific effective teaching strategies include the following:

- Using a "mental set" to motivate students to want to learn the material
- Breaking objectives into small steps (task analysis)
- Presenting clear information tied to objectives
- Modeling the use of skills being taught
- Using group and individual practice
- Constantly monitoring the progress of all students and making the necessary adjustment to ensure that all students master the lesson content

Example

The teacher begins the lesson by throwing the contents of the wastebasket on her desk, stimulating students' interest in the topic of archaeology. She then clearly states the objective and introduces the procedures of the lesson. She makes sure everyone has understood, making a point of calling on a range of students, not just on volunteers. When she is satisfied with comprehension, she then guides students' practice of the lesson (sometimes alone and sometimes in cooperative learning groups), moving around the room, asking questions, and monitoring each student's understanding of the material.

Cooperative Learning

This method for dividing students into mixed-ability learning teams has been widely recognized as a way to motivate students and teach both academic and social skills. It trains teachers to use research-based cooperative learning strategies known to increase student achievement. Teachers use cooperative learning groups to ensure mastery of the material by all students. Cooperative learning strategies include the following:

- Teaching positive social skills such as listening, helping, and sharing
- Creating heterogeneous learning teams

- Providing incentives for effective teamwork
- Providing opportunities for both formal and informal team-work
- Helping students work together toward mutual goals
- Rewarding group efforts, not just individual efforts
- Developing lesson plans that emphasize cooperation in student teams to master material

Example

Students traditionally spend half the school day working on their own. In this class, the children do their math assignment in teams of four, helping each other when they have difficulties. They ask each other questions during the math activity and summarize what they have learned, so that they are sure everyone in the group has mastered the concept. If all team members master the material, the team receives special recognition.

Cooperative learning addresses a crucial relationship between social skills and academic learning. Low academic achievement is a key risk factor for drug abuse, delinquency, and related problems. What is the relationship between academic achievement and such classroom activities as working with a team or learning positive social skills? According to research spanning more than two decades, the relationship is significant. Consider the following example:

The teacher has placed John in a group with three other children for reading practice, following instruction using interactive teaching techniques. Two of the others are strong readers, and the teacher knows John can benefit from working with them. But this requires that the group get along together — which means John must refrain from interrupting, teasing, and fooling around. The teacher realizes she cannot just place John in the group and tell the children to read together. First, it is necessary to teach the children *how* to work together and practice positive social skills like listening, sharing, and helping each other with the group task.

Teaching these skills requires direct instruction from the teacher as well as practice from students. When the children have learned how to work together, they will all benefit from the process. John is likely to improve both socially and academically. The other students will achieve at higher cognitive levels as they teach John and one another.

The teacher will accomplish several goals this way: John (and other high-risk students in the classroom) will learn both social and academic skills; John and other students will have more instructional time, which would not have been possible in a more traditionally structured classroom; John's group members will benefit by helping John; and heterogeneous grouping in the classroom will give all the students a chance to learn from each other and build new friendships.

Implementation

Instructional improvement programs center on the involvement and long-term commitment of the principal and teaching staff at each participating school, with support from key people at the district level. The principal's role has been found to be particularly crucial, since without administrative leadership and support, teachers will not be able to make or maintain changes in their instructional practices. Since long-term changes in schools are the ultimate goal of this element and change takes time, a school district commitment of at least three years is expected, after which the program should be institutionalized into ongoing practice.

Techniques and support materials are available to support each teacher's classroom management and teaching strategies. Teachers learn to incorporate these approaches into their basic repertoire and classroom style through training and in-building coaching and supervision.

Implementation Strategy

If a risk and resource assessment reveals school achievement or behavioral factors as a priority for action, the community board should form a task force to oversee the choice and implementation of institutional interventions. In addition to one or two members from the community board, the task force should include central office administrators, the director of staff development, principals, teachers, and representatives of the teachers' association for the districts involved. It is essential that one task force member be dedicated to the project at least one-quarter time for each participating school. Involvement of key personnel in decisions about how to proceed must occur at all levels of the schools and district. The project should be seen as an innovation in which teachers, principal, and district administration are cooperating to achieve action for risk reduction.

Implementation of this element will begin with the selection of the participating school or schools within the district. This is a critical step, since the principal and faculty at each participating school should be expected to make a long-term commitment to the project. Therefore, they need to have a clear understanding of what that commitment entails. At least half the teachers at each participating school should be expected to participate. Ideally, all the teachers at each school will be actively involved from the beginning. The principal at each school will be asked to make a major commitment to the project by coaching teachers on skills they have learned and, where several schools are involved, participating in regular meetings with other principals involved in this institutional change in instructional practice. Task force members should also work with local colleges and teacher training institutions to encourage incorporation of these instructional practices into teacher preparation curricula.

The Role of Peer Coaching

Research has repeatedly identified a weakness in teacher inservice training: a lack of transfer of knowledge and skills to the classroom. Further, some schools today lack adequate support and faculty collegiality to help teachers in implementing new methods. To overcome these difficulties, all participating teachers should learn peer coaching methods and be assisted in developing peer coaching programs at their schools (Cummings, 1985).

Peer coaching contrasts with "expert" coaching, because teachers help each other rather than being helped by another professional who is "above and beyond" day-to-day teaching responsibilities. It has the added advantage of becoming part of the school's continuing procedures, since the teachers themselves assume the responsibility for peer coaching. Unlike expert coaching, which may stop when program funding ends or a coach's position is eliminated, peer coaching can continue at the school indefinitely. Peer coaching also contributes to an atmosphere of heightened collegiality and professionalism in the school (Little, 1982). The peer coaching program should highlight (1) steps in peer coaching, (2) instruments to collect information for analysis of teaching, and (3) conferencing techniques.

When teachers have the opportunity to talk regularly about curriculum, classroom instruction, materials, testing, and so on, and to work as teams, they learn from each other. Teachers also learn from observing and being observed by each other. Outside professional support is important, too, especially if the perspective outsiders bring is one of current theory, research, and practice, and if they are clearly there to work *with* people, and not *on* them (Little, 1982).

Training and Technical Assistance

In-depth preparation and ongoing training and technical assistance are needed to implement this element successfully. Training is designed for groups of no more than thirty teachers at a time and is held on-site. Separate workshops for elementary, middle/junior high school, and high school faculty are desirable in larger districts with multiple schools involved. The full participation in training of the principal and/or vice principal from each school along with the teachers is key to the success of this element.

Workshops are available on proactive classroom management strategies, effective teaching strategies, cooperative learning, and peer coaching, as well as special sessions for principals, vice principals, central office staff development personnel, and district staff assigned to supervise and facilitate this program element. School districts implementing these instructional reforms should allow for twelve days of training over a two-year period for a minimum of half the staff of each participating school, three days of training for principals, and three days of training for district support staff.

Evaluation

Process Evaluation

One form of evaluation is regular observation of the participating teachers, using an instrument developed to measure time on task, teaching strategies, and student behavior. This can be used both as baseline data and as a diagnostic tool. An important goal in using an observational tool is to assist teachers in refining their skills and methods. Teachers should be trained in the use of the instrument as part of the peer coaching training. It is important to emphasize that the main purpose of such assessment is to refine teachers' skills and provide them with objective information about how they are doing — not to judge them. Throughout, self-improvement is an important focus.

Outcome Evaluation

Effects of instructional changes can be evaluated through examination of such available data as standardized achievement test scores, disciplinary records, referrals to the school office, attendance records, retention at grade level, and dropout rates. Also, survey instruments to assess students' attitudes toward school and their teachers are available.

Resources

For information on training, technical assistance, and evaluation tools for this program element, contact:

Developmental Research and Programs, Inc.
130 Nickerson, Suite 107
Seattle, WA 98109
Phone: (800) 736-2630

Institute for Research on Teaching
College of Education
Michigan State University
East Lansing, MI 48824-1034
Phone: (517) 353-6413

Robert E. Slavin
Center for Social Organization of Schools
The Johns Hopkins University
3505 N. Charles St.
Baltimore, MD 21208
Phone: (301) 516-0370

The W. T. Grant Consortium
on the School-Based Promotion
of Social Competence

Chapter 10

Drug and Alcohol Prevention Curricula

Overview

Most schools offer some form of drug education, yet research has shown that a great deal of drug education programming in the last two decades has had little or no impact. This element emphasizes new knowledge about well-researched approaches to school-based prevention programming, with an emphasis on programs that teach clearly identifiable *social competencies*. While not recommending specific prevention curricula, this chapter helps the community board make sound, research-based decisions about school curricula, using criteria developed by the W. T. Grant Consortium on the School-Based Promotion of Social Competence.

Children and youth at risk in kindergarten through twelfth

Note: Members of the W. T. Grant Consortium are Maurice J. Elias and Roger P. Weissberg, co-chairs; Kenneth A. Dodge, J. David Hawkins, Leonard A. Jason, Philip C. Kendall, Cheryl L. Perry, Mary Jane Rotheram-Borus, and Joseph E. Zins.

grade are reached through curricula provided to all students in these grades.

Problems/risk factors addressed in this chapter are early antisocial behavior, favorable attitudes toward drug use, academic failure, low commitment to school, alienation or rebelliousness, association with drug-using peers, and early first use of drugs.

Protective factors addressed in this chapter are bonding to school, skills to resist antisocial influences, and skills to establish positive social relationships.

Setting the Stage

Drug education and prevention programs in the schools are not a new idea. Virtually all states now require some form of drug education in grades K-12, and growing numbers of schools in recent years have adopted school-based prevention programs.

What makes ths element distinct from most other approaches to school-based prevention programming is its broadened vision of social competence promotion in schools and its emphasis on a rigorous and clearly defined process for choosing and implementing a program. At one time, simply adopting a curriculum to teach facts about drugs might have seemed sufficient. Much is now known, however, about which types of curricula are most effective and under what conditions they are most likely to be successful. Those criteria are spelled out in this chapter.

A key to effective school-based programming for drug abuse prevention highlighted in this chapter is social competence promotion. This approach goes beyond the conventional notion of drug education through teaching specific social and coping skills. Social competence promotion programs focus on four key skill areas: (1) self-management, (2) decision making and problem solving, (3) communication, and (4) resisting negative and limiting social influences. School-based programs that incorporate social competence promotion are promising for several reasons. They have been shown to be effective in a number of research and evaluation studies (see the Supporting Research section), and they are also consistent with the social development strategy.

Increasingly, promotion of social competence is being required as a component of comprehensive K-12 drug prevention and education programs. The 1989 amendments to the federal Drug-Free Schools and Communities Act, for example, require age-appropriate drug and alcohol programs that address the legal, social, and health consequences of drug use in grades K-12. In addition, the amendments require that programs teach effective techniques for resisting peer pressure to use illicit drugs or alcohol. State and local guidelines in many cases place an even stronger emphasis on social competence instruction. Community boards considering this element should be aware of the requirements that affect their local schools and recognize that social competence promotion often is no longer optional but essential.

Rationale

Once viewed as an "extra" with little relevance to the primary mission of schools, social competence promotion is increasingly recognized as a part of the basic educational process that enhances both social development and academic learning. There are many reasons for this shift in perspective. Children come to school from homes and communities that have changed radically in recent decades. Amid growing concerns about discipline, which has been rated the most serious problem of schools for more than a decade (Frymier & Gansneder, 1989), veteran teachers repeatedly note how the circumstances in which students find themselves have changed.

Where once skills and attitudes promoting self-discipline, problem solving, self-responsibility, effective communication, cooperation, and helping others might have been taught at home or through children's participation in the life of the community, now our communities are becoming increasingly fragmented and children are often isolated from positive social influences. Many children spend long parts of each day on their own, without the support and guidance of parents or other positive, caring adults (Cook, Howe, & Holliday, 1985; Perry, Kelder, & Komro, in press). Increasingly, negative peer influences fill the void (Bronfenbrenner, 1986). Perry et al. (in press) paint a stark picture:

Socialization for the '90s

The social environment of adolescents changed so
rapidly in the 1980s that it is difficult to ascertain
what "healthy" socialization should have been to prepare American youth for the 1990s. The most important microsystem, the family, appears to have
become increasingly impersonal and individualistic. . . . Overall, less adolescent time is spent with
parents or adults, more time is unsupervised. . . .
Correspondingly, greater influence of peer groups
and peer norms is seen . . . with potentially fright-
ening outcomes.

School curricula that focus on and support social competence promotion can help to counter this trend. At the primary
level, an appropriate focus is on basic social skills such as sharing, listening to others, and working cooperatively in a group.
As students mature, curricula should include a broader range
of skills, such as how to resist negative peer influences, solve
problems, set goals, and provide service to others. Throughout, social competence development programs support positive
social behaviors and values.

Curricula with a social competence emphasis not only
teach specific skills that help students to behave in responsible
and healthy ways. They also provide students with a sense of
self-efficacy, the feeling and confidence that they know how to
accomplish a particular goal and are able to accomplish it —
that the goal is within their power and reach. Such social strategies can be taught to all groups of students, no matter what their
racial/ethnic background or socioeconomic or at-risk status (Elias
& Weissberg, 1990, Jones, 1988; Kendall, Reber, McLeer,
Epps, & Ronan, 1990; Mirman, Swartz, & Barell, 1988; Palincsar & Brown, 1985; Presseisen, 1988).

Goals and Objectives

Goals

- To reduce early antisocial behavior, favorable attitudes
  toward drug use, academic failure, low commitment to

school, alienation or rebelliousness, association with drug-using peers, and early first use of drugs
- To promote bonding to school, skills to resist antisocial influences, and skills to establish positive social relationships

Objectives

- To implement effective, enduring programs for social competence promotion in the schools at all grade levels
- To teach all students skills for social competence—for example, assertiveness, self-discipline, impulse control, cooperation, communication, problem solving, and resisting negative influences
- To create a school environment that encourages students to practice social competence skills as part of the normal course of daily events

Supporting Research

Studies have found that social competence promotion in schools has a wide range of desirable effects. Among these positive outcomes are improved student behavior, more satisfied teachers, and decreased drug use and related health risks.

Through structured lessons, practice, and application, students at all grade and ability levels are able to learn social skills such as interpersonal problem solving and assertiveness and apply them in school (Aronson et al., 1978; Kendall & Broswell, 1982; Rotheram, 1982a, 1982b, 1987; Slavin, 1983; Spivack & Shure, 1989). Learning social skills has a positive effect not just on students' interactions with others but on their attitudes toward school, their interactions with teachers and other adults, and their academic achievement (Aronson et al., 1978; Rotheram, 1982a, 1982b). Finally, there is evidence that learning positive social behavior helps to "extinguish" negative and antisocial behavior (Caplan & Weissberg, 1989; Patterson, 1986; Stephens, 1978; Weissberg et al., 1981).

- *Teachers.* Teachers using social skills curricula are more satisfied with their classes and with teaching in general (Elias & Clabby, 1989; Forman, 1982; Rotheram, 1987).

- *Schools.* Schools that implement social competence promotion programs have fewer behavior problems and a more positive, cooperative school climate (Rotheram, 1982a, 1982b; Aronson et al., 1978).
- *Drug use and related health risks.* Social competence curricula are a promising form of school-based drug abuse prevention programming. Early experiments (in the late 1970s) showed that teaching students social skills was successful in reducing the onset of smoking among middle school students (Evans, 1976; Evans et al., 1981). More recently, social competence skills training has been used in programs that target the use of a wider range of drugs, including alcohol and marijuana. A number of studies have found that these programs have reduced students' intentions to use drugs or actual drug use for up to two and one-half years after the program (Ellickson & Bell, 1990; Flay et al., 1987; Johnson et al., 1989; Pentz, Dwyer, et al., 1989).

An important premise for social competence skills training in the context of alcohol and other drug use prevention is the ineffectiveness of approaches that focus just on conveying information about drugs or that teach general social skills without a specific emphasis on resisting negative influences. Such programs have been found to have little or no impact on students' drug use (Ellickson & Robyn, 1987).

Programs and curricula that promote the development of social competences can have a positive impact on many aspects of students' behavior and attitudes. It is unrealistic, however, to expect them to resolve serious emotional or behavioral problems. Simultaneous and/or coordinated referrals to more specialized programs will be needed for children whose behavior problems are beyond the scope of a prevention-oriented curriculum.

Program Description

Programs and curricula that focus on developing social competencies vary widely in structure and content from one grade level and developmental phase of childhood to another. Yet certain key principles should govern the selection of any social skills curriculum.

Social competency programs should focus on skill development. Programs that are only informational or that rely exclusively on textbooks and lectures may provide students with information about skills, but they do not promote the actual learning and use of those skills (Cartledge & Milburn, 1986). They should integrate skill teaching with the promotion of positive values and attitudes. Teaching a particular skill should not be regarded as an end in itself. Positive attitudes and values regarding that skill are also important. Effective social competence promotion programs promote values and attitudes that foster positive behaviors and interactions with others.

Effective instructional strategies must be provided. Skill development is the result of learning information about the skill, being exposed to modeling of the skill, practicing the skill, receiving feedback on use of the skill, and being reinforced for using the skill. This requires an interactive classroom format in which students participate in learning and trying out new skills and in which the use of those skills is encouraged and reinforced. The classroom is a kind of safe laboratory for development of skills that can then be used effectively outside the classroom (Allen, Chinsky, Larcen, Lochman, & Selinger, 1976; Combs & Slaby, 1977; Elias, 1990).

An accepting classroom climate is particularly important for effective social competence promotion (Damon, 1988; Elias & Clabby, 1989; Gilligan, 1987; Spivack & Shure, 1989). Openness and acceptance are needed in order to encourage students to try out skills that may seem unnatural or unfamiliar. The teacher in such a classroom needs to model the appropriate attitudes and ways of interacting with others. Changes in children's behavior can be slow. Social competence promotion requires most children, and many adults as well, to behave in new and different ways — working cooperatively together in groups, developing a sense of teamwork instead of purely individual achievement, listening to each other more carefully and sensitively, and helping each other.

Social competence requires the ability to adapt and integrate feelings (emotions), thinking (cognition), and actions (behavior) to achieve specific goals (Kendall, 1991). An emphasis on emotional, cognitive, and behavioral skills is therefore needed in the curriculum. The best programs combine skills training in all three areas in an integrated framework (Elias, 1990; Rotheram, 1982a). Criteria for selecting a social competence curriculum include determining that the curriculum addresses all three of these areas and explicitly teaches the following skills in each area.

Emotional Skills

- Identifying and labeling feelings
- Expressing feelings
- Assessing the intensity of feelings
- Managing feelings
- Delaying gratification
- Controlling impulses
- Reducing stress

Cognitive Skills

- Self-talk — conducting an "inner dialogue" as a way to cope with a topic or challenge or reinforce one's own behavior
- Reading and interpreting social cues — for example, recognizing social influences on behavior and seeing oneself in the perspective of the larger community
- Using steps for problem solving and decision making — for instance, controlling impulses, setting goals, identifying alternative actions, anticipating consequences, acting, and evaluating consequences
- Understanding the perspective of others
- Understanding behavioral norms (what is and is not acceptable behavior)
- A positive attitude toward life
- Self-awareness — for example, developing realistic expectations about oneself in order to predict one's own behavior

Behavioral Skills

- Nonverbal — communicating through eye contact, facial expressiveness, tone of voice, gestures, style of dress, and so on

- Verbal—making clear requests, responding effectively to criticism, resisting negative influences, expressing feelings clearly and directly, giving and receiving compliments
- Taking action—walking away from situations involving negative influences, helping others, participating in positive peer groups

Social competence promotion programs aim to change students' social behavior over the long term—improving the conduct of individual students, promoting more positive intergroup relations, and generally affecting the climate of the entire school in a positive way. This requires substantial support on the part of the school's administration, faculty, and parents, as well as the community. Many programs that teach social competence provide opportunities for participation in school events and other nonclassroom activities, for example, to extend the principles of social learning beyond the classroom and reinforce the program's basic philosophy (Elias & Weissberg, 1990; Hawkins & Catalano, 1990).

Parent involvement is critically important to the success of social competence programs. Parents should be informed and consulted as part of the curriculum selection process. In addition, programs should routinely offer opportunities for parents and their children to explore issues together, talk about and practice new skills the child is learning, or make changes in the home environment to support new skills (Pentz, Dwyer, et al., 1989; Perry, Pirie, Holder, Halper, & Dudovitz, 1990).

A number of studies have found peer leadership to be highly effective in school-based social competence programs at the secondary level (Klepp, Halper, & Perry, 1986; Tobler, 1986). Botvin and his colleagues found that peer leaders achieved greater reductions in substance use by student subjects than did classroom teachers (Botvin, Baker, Filazzola, & Botvin, 1990). The peer leadership results argue for including this component in secondary-level substance abuse prevention programs. Peer-led programs are also consistent with the emphasis of the social development strategy on providing opportunities for active involvement to promote bonding to school and on countering negative peer influences to use drugs. They help to establish and support a peer norm of no drug use.

The emotional, cognitive, and behavioral skills just described should be taught in social competence promotion programs offered consistently in grades K-12, following a clearly stated scope and sequence. This requires an understanding of which skills are most important at the various developmental stages. At each developmental level, the scope and sequence should focus on skills in five core areas: personal, family, peer group, school-related, and community-related.

A more variable but still necessary area includes topics that are event-triggered (skills needed to deal with events like death and divorce). Event-triggered curriculum components can be introduced at points where specific topics have been made important by events that have occurred in the lives of class members. They should focus on teaching all class members to be sensitive to and supportive of individuals experiencing the events; they should also aim at preventing unwanted ramifications of the event.

The competencies required to master the developmental tasks at each stage may be prerequisites for later development of more advanced and complex social competencies. If students are to achieve true competence in a given area, it is necessary for instruction to extend and elaborate on previous instruction in that area. For example, the content of the peer component of a curriculum in elementary school might focus on how to join groups of friends, but at the secondary level more emphasis might be placed on friendships across the genders.

Table 10.1 presents a suggested sequence and examples of competencies that could be included. Throughout, the emphasis is on core topics for teaching developmentally appropriate skills. The competencies are taught at stages of development where they are best suited to students' emotional, physical, and psychological readiness to learn them.

In summary, to be effective, school-based social competence programs should satisfy the following criteria:

The program must address identified needs and risk factors and be long term and coordinated, covering kindergarten through twelfth grade. It must involve parents and should involve peer leaders. It must employ effective instructional strategies to teach

Table 10.1. Social Competencies: Sequence and Examples.

	Grades K-2	Grades 3-5	Grades 6-8	Grades 9-10	Grades 11-12
Personal	Learning self-management Learning social norms about appearance washing face washing hair brushing teeth Recognizing drug warning labels	Understanding safety for latchkey kids interviewing people at door saying "no" to strangers or friends Knowing about healthy behaviors eating healthy foods helping family select healthy food exercising Managing time Being aware of sexual factors recognizing and accepting body changes recognizing and resisting inappropriate sexual behaviors	Recognizing the importance of alcohol and other drug abuse prevention establishing norms for health developing request and refusal skills acknowledging the importance of self-statements and self-rewards Being aware of sexual factors recognizing and accepting body changes recognizing and resisting inappropriate sexual behaviors	Taking care of self recognizing consequences of risky behaviors (sexual activity, drug use) Protecting self from negative outcomes—for example, safest (abstain) and less safe (for example, condoms, do not drink and drive) Earning and budgeting money Planning a career	Preparing for adult role living with others living alone making a home Planning a career
Family	Being in a family making a contribution at home—chores, responsibilities relating with siblings	Understanding families and different family forms and structures Being close—intimacy and boundaries	Recognizing conflict between parents' and peers' values—for example, in the areas of dress or importance of achievement Learning about stages in parents' (adults') lives	Becoming independent Talking with parents about daily activities learning self-disclosure skills	Preparing for parenting—family responsibilities

Table 10.1. Social Competencies: Sequence and Examples, cont'd.

	Grades K-2	Grades 3-5	Grades 6-8	Grades 9-10	Grades 11-12
Peers	Initiating conversations Being a member of a group sharing, taking turns cooperating	Expanding peer groups Learning to be close including and excluding others learning to set boundaries (secrets) Learning to cope with peer pressure to conform (dress) being assertive being self-calming Cooperating	Choosing friends Developing peer leadership skills Dealing with conflict among friends Recognizing and accepting alternatives to aggression	Initiating and maintaining cross-gender friends and romantic relationships practicing request skills practicing refusal skills	Understanding responsible behavior at social events and parties Dealing with drinking and driving
School-related	Following school rules Understanding similarities and differences—for example, skin color, physical disabilities Accepting responsibility in the classroom Respecting authority	Setting academic goals planning study time completing assignments Learning to work in teams Accepting similarities and differences—for example, appearance, ability levels	Learning skills for participating in setting policy Learning planning and management skills to complete school requirements Preventing truancy learning refusal skills setting personal norms/standards	Making a realistic academic plan recognizing personal strengths persisting to achieve goals in spite of setbacks Planning a career Participating in school service and other nonacademic involvement	Being a role model for younger students

Table 10.1. Social Competencies: Sequence and Examples, cont'd.

	Grades K–2	Grades 3–5	Grades 6–8	Grades 9–10	Grades 11–12
Community-related	Recognizing a pluralistic society being aware of holidays, different cultural groups, customs Accepting responsibility for the environment taking care of the classroom recycling	Joining groups outside of school Accepting cultural differences Helping people in need	Developing involvements in community projects Identifying and resisting negative group influences Accepting differences	Contributing to community service projects Accepting responsibility for the environment	Participating in community service or environmental projects Understanding elements of employment Understanding issues of government
Event-triggered	Coping with divorce Dealing with death in the family Becoming a big brother or sister to a sibling Dealing with family moves	Coping with divorce Dealing with death in the family Becoming a big brother or sister to a sibling Dealing with family moves	Coping with divorce Dealing with death in the family Dealing with a classmate's drug use or delinquent behavior	Coping with divorce Dealing with death in the family Dealing with a classmate's drug use or delinquent behavior, pregnancy, AIDS, suicide, and so on	Coping with divorce Dealing with death in the family Dealing with a classmate's drug use or delinquent behavior, pregnancy, AIDS, suicide, and so on

specific, developmentally appropriate social competencies — skills in managing feelings, thinking, and controlling behavior, and skills for resisting negative and limiting social influences.

The program should be coordinated with such intervention services as school guidance counseling, special education, student assistance programs, school clinics, and relevant community services. Instruction content should be tied to other subject areas, especially health and family life, but also academic subjects wherever possible.

Teachers must receive training in implementation methods and continuing support and technical assistance. Materials must be clear and up to date. The program should be designed to include methods for monitoring (1) implementation (process) with timely feedback and (2) goal-focused impact (outcome).

Any school-based social competence promotion program being considered by the task force responsible for this element should be assessed carefully using the guidelines in this chapter. Some of these guidelines might change over time, however. For example, the topics listed in Table 10.1 are appropriate for children in school in the early 1990s. There might have been less emphasis on discussion of sexuality and romantic relationships as recently as a decade ago. The epidemic of AIDS and the particular vulnerability of sexually active adolescents make some form of AIDS education, in conjunction with social competence teaching, imperative today.

Implementation

In recent years, schools throughout the country have widely adopted drug education programs or curricula. If the schools in your community already have drug education programs in place, community board members might be tempted to respond to this program element by saying, "We've already taken care of that." Instead, take a new look at the kinds of programs being implemented in local schools, and ask how well they achieve the objectives specified earlier in this chapter.

Effective implementation is schoolwide, coordinated, and long term. The school principal's leadership, commitment, and personal involvement are crucial to success. Parents and the community should be informed about the program, be involved in the selection process, and strongly support it. District administration should be well informed about the program and consider it a high priority. Teacher training to deliver the program is a key component, followed by some form of peer coaching. Program evaluation should be planned during initial implementation and should not be an "add-on." Remember that the program should be well integrated into the school curriculum, or it may be regarded as an afterthought.

This approach implies much more than just adopting a curriculum or exposing students to a few hours of drug information classes or a school assembly on drugs once a year. It is designed to integrate the promotion of social competencies into the daily activities and culture of the school, to make a long-lasting impact on students' attitudes and behavior (Commins, 1987; Elias & Weissberg, 1990; Perry et al., 1989). Implementation should progress through a series of well-planned stages involving broad representation from the school and community.

Taking Stock of Current Practice and Needs

A first step is to assess local schools' existing curricula in terms of the guidelines in the preceding section. Does the school district have a comprehensive prevention program in grades K-12? Are specific social competencies and skills being taught in the program? If the answer to either question is no, a new look at the schools' prevention programming is in order. These questions relate to the content of the program. Equally important are questions about how the program has been chosen and is being implemented.

Many school districts designate a committee of curriculum reviewers to assess currently available drug abuse prevention programs and make a selection. Often the choice is limited because districts have few resources for learning about programs. Programs are likely to be chosen in haste to meet state or local school board mandates. Increasingly, the experience of school districts throughout the country suggests that programs adopted and implemented in such a manner, without adequate planning and input from people at all levels of the school system, are likely to fail (Berman & McLaughlin, 1978; Comer, 1980; Weissberg, Caplan, & Sivo, 1989; DeFriese, Crossland, Pearson, & Sullivan, 1990; Gutkin & Curtis, 1990).

Selecting a Program

Ask the following questions before adopting a curriculum:

- In what districts or schools similar to yours has the curriculum been used, with what adaptations, and with what results?
- Can the program be implemented in your district without violating its integrity, that is, without significantly changing the design of the program?
- How well tested are the procedures for teacher training, particularly in situations similar to those in your school or district?
- Is the program approved by the Program Effectiveness Panel of the National Diffusion Network of the U.S. Department of Education or other authorities on effective programs of this kind?
- Is the program a comprehensive K-12 curriculum?
- Does the program have an adequate base in theory and research?
- Is it manageable for classroom teachers?
- Do teachers find it satisfying and valuable to use? Is it still used after the introductory period and the novelty wear off?
- Do students enjoy it?
- Is there controlled research data supporting its effectiveness?
- How well does this curriculum meet mandates already established by the state?
- How will it fit in with existing curricula?

A representative group of administrators, teachers, parents, students, and decision makers in the school and community should be involved in the selection of the program. At least one member of the panel should have experience in analyzing program research findings and impact data. From the beginning, the process also needs to have the understanding and support of the district administration. One option is to form a district-wide committee to study social competence promotion programs and recommend those that appear most appropriate.

Pilot Project

No matter what the size of the district, it is best to introduce a new program through a demonstration or pilot project. This provides opportunities to make modifications or adaptations, if necessary—or even to decide that the program is not appropriate for your particular setting. Assuming the pilot goes well, it also allows teachers to observe the program and thus gradually buy into it by talking with others who are enthusiastic about implementing it and eager to spread the word to colleagues. A careful evaluation process should be included as part of the pilot procedure to assess effectiveness, usefulness, and impact on identified risk and protective factors.

Teacher Recruitment

Teaching social competencies requires rapport with students, a relaxed and informal classroom atmosphere, and enthusiasm for the program's content. A strategy to generate this type of ownership is to encourage all interested teachers to observe the program in classrooms where it is being successfully implemented, to participate in training, and to support each others' efforts. As much as possible, an atmosphere of experimentation and collaboration should be encouraged—a spirit of "We're all in this together and it's okay to make mistakes." This can help to overcome the resistance that many teachers may feel toward such programs.

Integration with the School Curriculum

Ideally, social competence promotion will become a part of the school's core offerings. Many schools schedule lessons of this kind for a homeroom period. At the secondary level, courses with titles like "Life Skills" or "Social Living" are often required for at least one semester in junior high school and another in senior high school. Integrating a social competence promotion program with curricular offerings is only one step toward making it effective, however. The program also needs to be integrated with other continuing activities at the school. For example, if students are learning how to make responsible decisions in class, the school should support what they are learning by giving them increasingly responsible decision-making roles in the school itself.

Social competence programs are most effective when offered throughout grades K-12. How often children participate in classes or activities promoting social competencies will depend on a variety of factors, including the overall curriculum of the district, the available resources, and the presence of related programs such as cooperative learning.

A degree of intensity is necessary for these programs to be effective. Available evidence suggests that forty to sixty hours per year of instruction is associated with desired changes in students' health-related knowledge, attitudes, and behavior (Connell, Turner, & Mason, 1985). Since patterns of implementation will vary widely, however, the main criterion to keep in mind is the need for sustained, intensive programming, as opposed to superficial, "one-shot" delivery. Note that for students in special education classes, shortened, more frequent sessions are recommended.

Training and Technical Assistance

Training and site-based follow-up support will be critically important to the success of this component. Staff training should be offered by the developer of the chosen program or by an authorized trainer. The appropriate types of training and training formats vary from one program to another. To some extent, training needs depend on the prior experience level of staff in the school district with social competence promotion programs. Training of less than a full day is not likely to have much effect. Three to five days of training for a semester or year-long program is often necessary.

The training might take place in an intensive workshop before the beginning of the school year or in a series of one-day or afternoon workshops spaced throughout the school year. Training should provide an understanding of the conceptual and theoretical basis for the program and practice with actual program materials.

Follow-up support for at least a year after the initial training, preferably two to three years, is also important. It can be provided by the program developer's staff or trainers or curriculum specialists within the school district who have been trained by the program developer. Ideally, school-based monitoring and support will also be available through a peer coaching program (Elias & Weissberg, 1990).

Evaluation

Curriculum change requires sustained follow-up and support for its ultimate success. Initial implementation may show results, but they may not be as dramatic as one would hope. The task force's initial evaluation efforts should be directed toward assessing necessary levels of continuing support.

Process Evaluation

Areas to assess include the following:

- The number of teachers trained and the type of training provided
- The extent to which the whole program was delivered
- The integrity of the implementation—that is, faithfulness to the program design and materials
- How often teachers use the program or techniques in the classroom
- Annual consumer satisfaction evaluations by students and teachers

Outcome Evaluation

Central to assessment of the effectiveness of social competence promotion programs is measurement of the extent to which students acquire and actually use the skills being taught. Evaluation should focus on the specific skills taught at the various grade levels. Assessment tools are often provided by developers of curriculum packages and materials. Instruments should assess not just knowledge and use of skills but students' sense of self-efficacy and attitudes toward using those skills, an essential part of an individual's motivation to use new skills after learning them.

Other measures of program impact include data available from school records and self-reports of grades, absenteeism, tardiness, and disciplinary referrals. Also important are data on student drug use, peer pressure, attitudes toward alcohol and other drugs, and perception of peers' use. The early, continuous, and rigorous implementation of social competence promotion curricula in the schools should contribute to the reduction of drug abuse risks and increase skills important in protecting against drug abuse.

Resources

The following resources are available as aids in identifying and selecting programs:

Carnegie Council on Adolescent Development. (1989, March). *Teaching Decision Making to Adolescents: A Critical Review.* Washington, DC: Carnegie Council on Adolescent Development.

Health Promotion Resource Center, Stanford Center for Research in Disease Prevention. (1989). *What Works: A Guide to School-Based Alcohol and Drug Abuse Prevention Curricula.* Stanford, CA: Stanford Center for Research in Disease Prevention.

U.S. Department of Education. (1988). *Drug Prevention Curricula: A Guide to Selection and Implementation.* Washington, DC: U.S. Government Printing Office.

Chapter 11

Community and School Drug Use Policies

Overview

This program element offers insight into the power and process of policy making. It is designed for those in the community who are interested in working to change aspects of the environment that contribute to the use of alcohol and other drugs. Policy can be a vital and effective tool for positive changes at all levels of a community, whether the community begins with a campaign to get a particular store to stop selling alcoholic beverages to minors or spearheads an initiative to raise the tax on alcohol statewide. Policy activities require broad-based community support and an understanding of the issues' complexity and context. This program element offers a basic understanding of the issues. It also provides guidance in the development, revision, coordination, and implementation of community and school policies. Policy changes can affect the whole community and people of all ages.

Problems/risk factors addressed in this chapter are community attitudes favorable to alcohol and other drug use; availability of alcohol and other drugs; and use and problem patterns of use among friends or family.

Protective factors addressed in this chapter are clear antialcohol and other drug norms and attitudes; bonding to communities and schools that have positive norms and policies regarding alcohol and other drugs; opportunities to become involved in community and school programs consistent with positive norms; skills to implement policies; and recognition and reward for participation in the policy-making process.

Setting the Stage

Policies are laws, rules, codes, or standards that guide people's behavior and their interactions with their environment. Policies are made at all levels: individual, group, local community, state, federal, and international. This chapter describes the potential for counteracting alcohol and other drug problems through the development and reinforcement of policy within the community and the school. It gives examples of some of the concrete, positive changes that can take place when communities and schools mobilize to design and implement effective policies.

The recognition that alcohol and other drug problems are a community responsibility places them in a broad context that includes social, political, cultural, economic, and physical influences. Community and school policies are critical elements of comprehensive prevention programs, for they have the power to influence the behavior of individuals and affect the welfare of the total community.

Policy change involves taking collective action. It means challenging accepted practices, norms, and the status quo regarding alcohol and other drug use. It requires developing new coalitions and constituencies as well as new skills. Working with policy issues helps to clarify current community norms and practices that may contribute to alcohol and other drug problems.

Rationale

Laws, rules, and other forms of policies are governing principles or guidelines for behavior. Each level of government has specific roles and responsibilities with regard to policy making.

For example, in the case of alcohol, tax policy has historically been set at the federal and state levels. The federal government has the prime responsibility for regulating advertising and production, although states are the primary determiners of physical availability. States determine the extent of local control and set the parameters for local action. As a community board begins to look at the possibilities for policy change or the development of new policy, they must know where the targeted policies originate, so that the appropriate agencies, organizations, institutions, or individuals can be petitioned and involved.

Most of the decisions made within a community are common agreements, usually unwritten, about what constitutes acceptable behavior. These agreements are called social norms and standards. They range from family norms to informal neighborhood norms to shared expectations for behavior among teenagers. Norms are often translated into explicit policies and laws. For example, increasingly in some parts of the United States, cigarette smoking at social events is considered unacceptable behavior. This antismoking norm has been embodied in laws governing smoking in airplanes and public buildings. Norms regarding alcoholic beverages are also changing. Growing awareness of the problems associated with alcohol drinking has led to stricter laws regarding driving under the influence, higher minimum drinking ages, and neighborhood organizing against billboard advertising, among other policies and actions.

Ideally, written, codified or "formal" policies reflect a community's values or social norms. They are a clear expression of which behaviors or ideas the majority of the people deem important — and also those that a minority of people might not follow on their own. If everyone agreed about certain behaviors or courses of action, there would be no need to formulate laws, rules, or policies. Further, for policies to be accepted and followed, norms and policies should be closely aligned. A formal policy is not only a guideline for behavior. It also implies or explicitly states consequences for those who do not abide by the policy. If a restaurant has a no-smoking policy, a diner who lights up will be asked to put the cigarette out or leave the restaurant. If there is no explicit policy and the hostess merely says as she seats you that the restaurant prefers that you not smoke, then to smoke or not to smoke is still left to the diner's discretion.

Written policies (rules and laws) generally govern the use of legal substances in the community and clearly state which substances are illegal to use and under what conditions. Federal, state, and local laws figure importantly in these policies. Examples include controls on the location and number of places that sell alcoholic beverages, the type of outlet (for example, quick-serve gas station versus state-controlled store), and whether or not alcohol is allowed at public events. Although schools are bound by community laws, most have their own written policies regarding the use of alcohol and other drugs on campus. As is the case with norms and policies generally, school and community policies must be congruent or there will be confusion about the standards of behavior within a community. If there is too great a difference between policies at the school and community level, a mixed message is communicated that may imply a choice in how people should behave.

Unwritten or informal policies are often at least as important as the law itself in influencing behavior norms. The manner in which policies are enforced or not creates unwritten policy. Examining the enforcement of formal policies offers insight into the actual standards of acceptable behavior or social norms. Are drug laws strongly enforced in low-income neighborhoods but ignored in middle-class, white-collar areas? Does the school have a clear "no use on campus" policy that is regularly ignored? If so, the school's unwritten policy is to ignore the written one. Whatever the reason for it, selective, inconsistent enforcement is a form of unwritten policy. It is important that communities and schools understand the need to make policies explicit and appropriate, and then to enforce them with specific consequences or reinforce them with incentives. Policies that are unwritten, unclear, unenforced, or not reinforced can contribute to alcohol and other drug problems.

Conflicts between policies and people's actual behavior often reflect a lack of clarity about existing policies or a lack of understanding of the difference between written and unwritten policies. For example, the community has a policy not to serve alcohol to anyone under twenty-one. Schools, local licensing officials, and many parents try to enforce this rule. How-

ever, some parents do not, and they sponsor keg parties. A local festival does not check the identification of those served alcoholic beverages. Local merchants regularly do not check identification, and local employers serve underage employees. The
local police do not consider these infringements of policy to be
a high priority for law enforcement. Alcohol producers target
teenagers with slick ads, and tax policy is such that beer is as
cheap as soft drinks. Conflicts like these rise when policies are
not consistent at all levels. This type of conflict threatens the
effectiveness of policy in drug abuse prevention efforts.

It is essential to distinguish between adult policy and youth
policy, since differences often create yet another area of conflict.
School policies are youth-oriented by definition. Community
policies usually specify the legal use of some substances by adults
(most notably, alcohol), prohibiting use by minors. An important part of assessing and defining a community's drug-related
policies is to acknowledge that policies designed for adults will
inevitably have an effect on children and youth as well, for they
establish the community alcohol and other drug "environment."
Community norms shape the expectations and behavior of
youth. It may be acceptable and legal for adults to drink alcohol at picnics in public parks, for example. Yet this is the type
of policy the community may wish to reexamine as it becomes
more aware of the impact of drinking in public parks on the
alcohol and other drug-using behaviors of high-risk youth.

Central to "Communities That Care" is an emphasis on
comprehensiveness: the development of consistent policies across
families, schools, and communities that incorporate the social
development strategy. In addition to written policies, the content and methods of programs aimed at reducing drug-related
risk factors are themselves a concrete embodiment of community policies. Indirectly, they constitute policy "statements."

Goals and Objectives

Goals

- To alter community norms that promote the abuse of alcohol and other drugs

- To reduce availability of alcohol and other drugs for young people
- To promote clear antidrug community norms and attitudes
- To promote bonding to communities and schools that have positive norms and policies regarding alcohol and other drugs

Objectives

- To assess the current drug and alcohol policies of a community and its schools
- To identify specific and consistent policies communities and schools can implement to reduce the risk that children and adolescents will use drugs
- To mobilize the community at a variety of levels, ranging from established leaders to neighborhood advocates, in order to assess, analyze, refine, and implement consistent, comprehensive policies related to alcohol and other drug use.

Supporting Research

There is a consensus among researchers that for policies to be effective, they must be comprehensive, addressing a wide range of environments and drug-related behaviors; reasonable, including clear but not overly punitive consequences; and consistently communicated and implemented (Hawley, Petersen, & Mason, 1986; Pentz, Brannon, et al., 1989; Moskowitz, 1989). Effective policies also convey clear messages regarding no use of illegal drugs by anyone and no use of alcohol by minors. They state the consequences of use (Goodstadt, 1986), and they identify ways to reward and reinforce the decision not to use drugs.

School Policies

Although most schools have drug policies, the way policies are developed and implemented varies widely. One study (Moskowitz, 1983) compared school policies among a large number of schools with varying reports of alcohol and other drug problems among students. Schools that reported fewer student alcohol and other drug problems shared the following characteristics:

most faculty rigorously enforced their school's alcohol and drug policy, fewer alcohol retail outlets were located within a half mile of the school, and smoking by students at school was prohibited. This same study found that school discipline policies controlled problem behaviors more effectively when the faculty were trained to implement the policy, referred students with problems for help, and were supported by local courts and police. Schools in which the faculty, parents, and students supported the principal in implementing the policy and in which due process procedures were followed reported fewer behavior problems overall.

A review of middle and junior high school smoking policies found that schools emphasizing prevention approaches over cessation had reduced levels of smoking violations. Punitive measures, including the severity of consequences for violation, did not affect smoking rates (Pentz, Brannon, et al., 1989). A study of students' attitudes toward punishment in school settings (Grasmick & Bryjak, 1980) found that the perceived certainty of punishment for violations of school rules was far more important than the perceived severity of punishment. Explicit requirements of a school policy need to be balanced by drug education that helps students internalize or "buy into" the norms established by the policy (Goodstadt, 1989).

Community Policies

Research on community policies has been focused primarily on alcohol use and availability. Policy issues now dominate the alcohol field, and policy approaches are widely considered to be a critical part of a comprehensive program to prevent alcohol-related problems. The general thrust of alcohol-related policies in recent years has been to limit the availability of alcohol, particularly sales of alcohol to minors, and to strengthen penalties for illegal or irresponsible use of alcohol.

Consumption of alcoholic beverages has declined significantly in the last decade throughout the country, and public sentiment is increasingly anti-alcohol. This is not, however, as some representatives of the alcoholic beverage industry have claimed, the new Prohibition. Rather than calling for outright prohibition, discussions of alcohol policy have focused on several key areas: availability of alcohol outlets, minimum-age drinking laws, and price (Grossman, Coate, & Arluck, 1987; Mosher, 1985). Moreover, there is a fundamental difference in perspective between the Prohibition movement and the current public health approach. As one expert observes,

> The public health perspective does not seek to fundamentally alter human nature, and relies on legislation and regulation, as well as education, to limit consumption generally in order to control the scope of alcohol problems. . . . The increased use of taxation, the regulation of the hours of sale, the setting of age limits, advertising restrictions, or the control of the number of liquor outlets smacks of Prohibition. . . . But the mistake of Prohibition was to confuse protecting the community and the common life with legislating an official lifestyle [Beauchamp, 1985, pp. 29, 34].

Program Description

The community and school policy element incorporates a wide range of policy-making strategies. All have been implemented successfully in a variety of settings. Here we present a number of policy areas and related activities on which a community board might focus, in the community at large and in the schools.

Community Policies

Communities with high densities of alcohol outlets have higher rates of alcohol consumption and more long-term alcohol-related problems. Communities can affect local *availability* through zoning and planning laws that prohibit the sale of alcoholic beverages in areas frequented by high-risk youth and by the regulation of hours and days of sale, including sales at public events.

To illustrate, an alcohol policy campaign in Santa Clara County, California, resulted in the adoption of a comprehensive local zoning ordinance requiring more careful review of proposed new alcohol outlets. In response to car crashes caused by "happy hour" attendees, communities in Massachusetts enacted local regulations that banned happy hours at local bars and restaurants. The creation of "drug-free zones" within a certain radius of schools can also affect availability. Another approach to reducing availability of tobacco to children has been the removal of cigarette vending machines from public places.

Availability can also be affected by activities such as neighborhood "drug watches" similar to crime watches, in which local residents work closely with the police to identify and report illegal drug activities. A number of communities have found that a process of "reclaiming," in which a park or housing project is cleaned up and used by residents for alcohol- and other drug-free gatherings, helps to reduce the availability of illicit drugs. In Philadelphia, community activists, with police help, harassed drug dealers, boarded up crack houses, and, with a growing community coalition, organized all-night vigils on the streets of their neighborhood to keep the dealers away.

Raising the minimum drinking age from eighteen to twenty-one has reduced youthful fatal traffic crash rates by an estimated 25 to 30 percent. However, enforcement of the ban on sales to minors varies from one community to another, and enforcement is critical to the success of these laws. *Responsible beverage service* can dramatically affect the availability of alcohol to teens. Legal responsibility should be enforced among adults who serve or sell alcohol to minors or who promote drunkenness among adults, which affects community norms. Several communities in California, working with local law enforcement officials, have substantially reduced sales to minors by conducting "sting" operations at local alcohol outlets. Those operators found to be selling to minors were encouraged to attend special seminars on responsible beverage service. Similar operations have been launched for sales of tobacco products to children and youth.

Communities can address the serving of alcohol to minors in many other ways. For example, alcohol is often available to all at community events, at corporate family picnics, and at parent-sponsored keg parties. An effective countermeasure could be to promote and organize alcohol- and other drug-free community events.

Policies that affect the *pricing* of alcoholic beverages can reduce adolescent use, for young people tend to be very price-sensitive. Even modest increases in excise taxes have been found to have at least as great an effect on adolescent drinking as increases in the legal drinking age (Grossman et al., 1987). According to Mosher (1985), the appropriate use of excise taxes is the most neglected and possibly the most effective policy tool available to the public for the prevention of youthful drinking problems. Many states have raised alcohol excise tax rates in recent years in response to both budget crises and popular initiatives that have supported the public health benefits of such a policy.

Increasingly, alcohol abuse prevention experts are looking at ways in which alcoholic beverage *marketing and advertising* are targeted at youth—through promotion of sports events, featuring well-known athletes and musicians in advertising, special youth-oriented advertising supplements, and other methods (Mosher, 1985). Beer ads, for example, seek to make beer an integral part of the rite of passage for teenage boys (Postman, Nystrom, Strate, & Weingartner, 1988). Other ads specifically target African-American and Hispanic communities—billboards advertising alcohol and tobacco proliferate in inner city neighborhoods. Laws governing the advertising, marketing, and sale of alcoholic beverages can be an important component of a comprehensive drug policy, including the requirement of warning labels and signs in places that sell alcoholic beverages.

Community activity against advertising has focused primarily on billboards that target low-income, minority communities. In New York City and Dallas, billboards have been painted over in protest. In Wayne County, Michigan, community leaders targeted a particular billboard advertiser and sent a letter insisting that the offending billboards be removed. The letter listed ways in which the community would respond if the demand was not heeded, including encouraging every community organization to boycott the advertised products, picketing the company's facilities, and publicizing the issue throughout the media. Within one month of this coordinated campaign, every billboard was removed (McMahon & Taylor, 1990).

Budgeting is actually one of the most important forms of policy making for the prevention of adolescent substance abuse in a community. Do budgets place a high priority on prevention, in contrast to treatment or law enforcement? Do they provide for a wide range of positive involvements for high-risk youth? Close examination of local government and health agency budgets can lead to policy development that might affect a community's risk and protective factors.

Some other useful strategies include building coalitions of youth-serving agencies to define consistent alcohol and drug policies and monitoring state and federal legislation and programs to determine the results of efforts similar to those being contemplated in the community.

School Policies

Schools are, on the one hand, self-contained environments that have a significant influence on students simply because they spend so much time at school among their peers. On the other hand, schools do not exist in isolation and must be well integrated into the larger community. These facts have particular significance for establishing school policies.

Especially important to the successful development and implementation of school policies are clarity, consistency, and coordination. There should be a strong "no-use" message combined with an emphasis on health promotion. It is important to design ways of making the policy known throughout the school and community, including periodic updates. There should also be a clear rationale for school policies, including a statement of philosophy and goals. Policies must be consistent, within the school itself and between the school and the community. This means working closely with members of both to coordinate school and community policies.

Appropriate *curriculum* such as a K-12 social competence promotion curriculum, including drug information, social competencies, and training in skills for resisting peer and negative influences, can help to reinforce both the rationale for the policy and its implementation. *Training for teachers* in the rationale and effective implementation of policy and prevention programs in the school is another aspect of effective policy implementation. Teachers should understand the many ways they can support policy to make it effective.

Policy should be supported by clear and appropriate *consequences* for using alcohol or other drugs on campus and at school-sponsored functions off campus. It is important to coordinate the implementation of consequences with parents and others in the community. A related issue is *due process*. There should be steps for informing the principal, parents, and the police; for referring students with alcohol or other problems to treatment; and for following through with suspension or expulsion, if appropriate. Those who behave appropriately should receive *rewards and recognition;* mechanisms must be in place to see that this happens.

A crucial step in developing or refining a school drug policy is determining who will be involved and how decisions about the policy will be made. Part of the success of a school policy will depend on how it is developed by students, parents, and community members. Students, particularly high-risk youth, are more likely to abide by the policy if they are involved in its development. Some of the most effective school policies have been developed by coalitions of parents, students, and educators.

How might a school policy regarding alcohol and other drug use address risk and protective factors? One example might be a policy to encourage *peer norms* favoring nonuse of alcohol and other drugs. Communities and schools often think of alcohol and other drug-related policies in terms of "getting tough on drugs" or "making it clear we won't tolerate alcohol and other drugs here." That can and should be an important part of an alcohol and other drug-use policy. Just as important, however, is the need to consider positive alternatives to alcohol and other drug use: for example, activities and involvement that offer high-risk youth a compelling reason not to use alcohol and other drugs.

Through an emphasis on drug-free social and sports events, continually reinforced by effective policy enforcement and antidrug messages, the school administration can encourage students to reject drug-using peer groups and negative peer influences. For example, alcohol (and other drug)–free parties, including elaborate graduation night events, have been carried out in school districts throughout the country. The social development strategy suggests that we think about making our community a place where young people know there will be serious consequences for using alcohol and other drugs—but also where they will not want to use them because they have more rewarding and satisfying things to do. The entire community and school environment needs to provide support for the youth's decision to stay drug-free. The impact of the policy should be periodically assessed through anonymous assessments of students' attitudes.

Implementation

The choice of which policies to pursue varies from one community to another. The process of choosing begins with an assessment and analysis of existing policies in both the community and schools to identify gaps and inconsistencies. This involves mobilizing people and groups across the community and will be integral to the initiation of the "Communities That Care" strategy in a community. Once an assessment and analysis of existing policies has been done, the policy task force can determine priorities.

Establishing a Policy Task Force

Members of the task force for this program element should be people who are willing and able to work in a highly collaborative way with others. They will need to develop a broad range of skills: organizing, political advocacy, writing, legal, and negotiation skills, for example. The task force should broadly represent the schools and community. Members might include representatives of local service agencies, parents, educators, religious leaders, and health and media professionals. Youth participation is particularly important in this element.

Beyond its own membership, the task force should involve as many participants as possible in the assessment and policy-making process and should minimize competition between the task force and existing groups. If, for example, a grassroots group has taken action to eliminate crack houses in a particular neighborhood, representatives of that group might be invited to meet with the task force to address specific aspects of community policy related to their experience. Other school and community groups might be invited to participate in a similar manner. This will help to build bridges within the community, mobilize and gain the support of a greater percentage of the community, and facilitate access to information about what is already being done and what further needs the community might have.

It is important to note that the public health goals of the task force may conflict with some local business interests, especially those involved in the sale of alcoholic beverages. It would be inappropriate to have representatives of such businesses on the task force. Members should be prepared for conflicts that might arise when they call for policies that are problematic for these businesses.

Assessing Existing Policies

Assessing existing policies is one of the first tasks to be undertaken, since it provides a context and a foundation for the task force's work. In determining what already exists, what has worked, and what has not been effective, the task force can determine what steps to take next. Assessment requires gathering data by interviewing key informants and following through on other research required to get the facts.

Here are some examples of specific community policy assessment questions to ask:

- *Availability.* Where are alcoholic beverages available? How many outlets are there, and what are their business hours? Are there outlets near schools? Do proprietors regularly ask young people for identification? Are some parents known to serve minors in their homes?
- *Advertising.* How are alcohol and tobacco advertised? Are

there enticing billboards? Is the advertising in the community aimed at youth or high-risk populations? Are other messages that counter alcohol and other drug use communicated throughout the community?

- *Consistency.* Is the content and enforcement of existing alcohol and other drug policies and laws consistent across organizations within the community, including schools? Are there differing standards for alcohol and other drug use among different subgroups in the community?
- *Positive alternatives.* Are alternatives to alcohol and other drug use available for high-risk youth? Are there alcohol- and other drug-free social events, organizations, and adolescent "rites of passage"? Do adults have alcohol- and other drug-free ways to relieve stress and enjoy themselves?
- *Accountability.* Are there clear systems of due process and consequences for not adhering to policies? Are these consistently enforced throughout the community?

These questions should be asked with regard to school policy:

- *Clear messages.* Are schools' policies stated clearly in a published form and shared routinely with students and parents? Is a nonuse message reinforced with clear consequences for possessing, selling, or using alcohol and other drugs? Does the policy apply to student use of alcohol and other drugs both on and off campus? In existing written school policies is prevention emphasized, rather than surveillance or treatment?
- *Faculty.* Does the policy address alcohol and other drug use by teachers? Do teachers receive appropriate alcohol and other drug education and other resources to enable them to implement school policy?
- *Accountability.* Does the school keep parents informed of any attendance, academic, and social problems, including alcohol and other drug problems, that their children might have and work with them to resolve these issues?

Tools for assessing and changing existing policies are available and can be obtained by contacting the Resources listed at the end of this chapter.

Revising or Setting Policies

Once the policy task force has gathered enough information regarding existing policies, the group can come together to conduct a comprehensive review, identifying inconsistencies (particularly between community and school), gaps, and the need for any new policy initiatives. New or revised policies should meet certain standards endorsed by the community board: policies should address the risk factors for drug use among children and adolescents, and they should be developed so that those affected believe in and are committed to them.

Establishing new or revised policies, if necessary, is a logical outgrowth of the assessment process. The task force members should be aware that at this stage of the process they may meet with resistance from the community's current political structure, the school's administration, representatives of the alcohol industry, and others who are satisfied with the status quo. It is a good idea to remember that policies can be developed at many different levels, in many different institutions, and in a great variety of situations. It is wise to tackle "winnable battles" first.

New or revised policies must be announced and publicized. Such policies cannot be effective without high visibility and broad support (Mosher & Jernigan, 1989). One way to achieve this is to hold a public forum or a series of forums as part of the policy development process. Events like these should include representatives of all segments of the community and receive wide exposure in the local media. They can be combined with a related media campaign. Part of the process should include ways to incorporate input about the policies, with specific mechanisms for gathering the opinions and ideas of community members in reaction to proposed changes.

Working closely with the media is an essential part of the process. The policy task force can identify problem areas and issues for news stories or television specials that will broaden awareness and concern and provide wider support for action. Because of the need for broad community involvement, this program element complements the media element (Chapter Twelve), which will offer ways to involve media representatives.

Monitoring the implementation of revised or new policies is an important activity to ensure new policies are carried out and new programs established. It might include following through to see if teachers are consistently enforcing school policies or checking to see that gas stations are not selling alcohol. Monitoring policies and revising them in response to new developments will be a continuing activity of the policy task force.

Rewarding the Positive

The social development strategy stresses the role of recognition in increasing commitment. Yet there are few existing mechanisms for recognition for simply obeying the law or "doing the right thing," either in schools or the community. The task force should therefore focus on the development of recognition as one part of its implementation process. In a school where drug problems are few or where the situation has clearly improved, those positive accomplishments should be explicitly recognized. The policy task force might organize a communitywide program to recognize alcohol and drug-free schools and provide specific positive alternatives or recognition for the youth involved. Accomplishments throughout the community should be recognized and rewarded as well — the bar that drops its "happy hour," the parents that plan alcohol- and drug-free graduation nights, and the neighbors who clean up a "users" park all should be publicly recognized.

Training and Technical Assistance

Many community people already have the motivation to develop and enforce policy, but they do not necessarily have the tools — the techniques and strategies — to do so. Training in community policy will (1) give participants an introduction to the techniques and strategies for effective policy making and (2) develop a sense of bonding and empowerment among people who are interested in effecting change in their communities. The training for this element includes conducting assessments, developing policies, and organizing for effective policy implementation. For more specialized aspects of policy development and implementation, communities will need to work with a policy consultant.

Community Policy Training

The groups involved in assessing and analyzing policies may be different from those involved in revising, setting, and implementing them, and so different groups may need to be trained at different stages of the process. Communities that choose to initiate policy change should identify representatives to receive training, and then arrange for training to be provided by one of the groups listed in the Resources section at the end of the chapter. Some of the content areas to be covered in training include the following:

- Historical perspectives on alcohol and other drug-related problems
- Assessing the alcohol and other drug environment
- Overview of policy options
- Developing strategies for changing norms and policies around alcohol and other drug use
- Team building and coalition building for local action (community organizing principles)
- Alcohol availability
- Alcohol taxation as a policy strategy
- How the media will be involved with actions to change community norms and formal policies

School Policy Training

Separate training is available for task force members who are focusing on school policy issues. A one-day training has been developed by the American Council for Drug Education, and its content is based on their "Seven Steps" program. Here are their seven steps for developing a no-use school policy on alcohol and other drugs:

1. Understand chemical dependency — insight into the physical and psychological effects of alcohol and other drug use, with an emphasis on the "contagious" nature of abuse

2. Assess needs — determine the aspects of the problem that are unique to that location
3. Determine the direction policy should follow — based on the needs, find a particular course of action for the school to take
4. Compare past and present policies with a "no-use" alcohol and other drug policy — evaluate how effectively current policies meet the newly assessed needs
5. Align needs with resources — determine if the school has the necessary staff and/or volunteers to meet the needs
6. Specify and implement the policy — involve parents and representatives from community organizations relevant to the welfare of children in the development of policy; apply policy in a coordinated and continuous manner throughout the school years
7. Evaluate and update policy — determine through specific questions if the policy is achieving its intended goals and make adjustments accordingly

As these action steps for school policy change indicate, evaluating the policy's implementation and effects is an essential part of the process of using policy change for risk reduction.

Evaluation

Process Evaluation

Indicators of ways in which this element is implemented adequately include the following:

- Participation of key representative of different sectors of the community
- Number and breadth of policies being assessed, revised, or developed, including how comprehensive they are in covering a variety of social institutions and settings
- Occurrence of public events focusing on policy, including who and how many people participate
- Consistency of school policy enforcement
- Documentation of comprehensive and consistent policies across organizations serving children and youth — schools, service agencies, clubs, and so on

- Occurrence of public forums or meetings on policy issues and media presentations (newspaper articles, television news broadcasts or specials) referring specifically to policy issues

Outcome Evaluation

Indicators of the effectiveness of new, existing, or revised policies include the following:

- Decrease in the number of alcoholic beverage outlets near schools or billboards advertising tobacco or alcohol
- Change in patterns of drug use and attitudes toward drug use among youth
- Improvements in school attendance, lateness, dropout rates, and student achievement
- Increases in the number of alcohol-free events or neighborhood groups working with local police to deter drug selling
- Decreases in alcohol- or drug-related car crashes
- Changes in patterns of drug use and attitudes toward drug use
- Decreases in alcohol sales to minors

Changes in community and school policies can significantly alter the availability of both alcohol and other drugs, and create norms and standards that protect against drug abuse.

Resources

For training and technical assistance in developing and implementing school policy change, contact:
American Council for Drug Education
204 Monroe St., Suite 110
Rockville, MD 20850
Phone: (301) 294-0600

A leading resource for alcohol-related policy information and initiatives is the Center for Science in the Public Interest. Contact:

Center for Science in the Public Interest
1501 16th St., N.W.
Washington, DC 20036
Phone: (202) 332-9110

An approach to prevention policy development appropriate for many settings, including schools, has been developed by the Marin Institute of San Rafael, California. Two tiers of training are currently offered twice each year through the University of California at San Diego Extension Programs. These include a two-day introductory curriculum and a four-day follow-up residential program including advanced skill building, community organization, and media advocacy. Tailoring of this training for individual communities is also possible. Contact:
James Mosher, Ph.D.
Marin Institute
1040 "B" Street, Suite 300
San Rafael, CA 94901
Phone: (415) 456-5692

For information about policy training available from the federal Office for Substance Abuse Prevention, contact:
National Clearinghouse for Alcohol and Drug Information
Office for Substance Abuse Prevention
P.O. Box 2345
Rockville, MD 20852
Phone: (800) 729-6686 or (301) 468-2600

Chapter 12

Media Mobilization

Overview

The communications media in a community are in a particularly strong position to provide visibility and create a favorable environment for any comprehensive strategy focusing on alcohol and other drug use. Media task force members need to educate the local media about the ways children are placed at high risk of drug abuse and what protective actions can be taken. In addition, task force members should learn how to work with local media to develop coordinated, long-term campaigns that promote standards opposing the use of alcohol, tobacco, and other drugs by youth. Media campaigns can reach all segments of the community and people of all ages.

Problems/risk factors addressed in this chapter are favorable community attitudes toward alcohol and other drug use. Media efforts can also target specific risk factors addressed by other program elements adopted by the community board.

Protective factors addressed in this chapter are community bonding; clear norms against drug use; opportunities for community involvement; and recognition of positive behaviors, activities, and accomplishments.

Setting the Stage

Media mobilization can complement and support all the other elements of a comprehensive risk reduction campaign. Enlisting the media as advocates for prevention means working closely with media representatives to spread the word about innovative approaches to alcohol and other drug problems and the accomplishments of the community's risk reduction effort. In this way, the media can be used to heighten awareness, activate community support, and participate in prevention activities. Further, this approach can influence widespread changes in community attitudes, norms, and values regarding the issue of alcohol and other drugs. Media mobilization has much in common with the community and school drug use policy element, and the two elements can complement each other.

This element uses effective approaches to working with local media. It creates a two-way exchange of information and support: (1) the community board works with and educates the media about drug abuse prevention to create a communitywide climate of advocacy for community change, and (2) the media receive opportunities for stories, features, and other forms of coverage of a topic with broad audience appeal.

The media campaign developed as part of "Communities That Care" involves a wide range of approaches, a research-based model for community change, and the long-range goal of making the whole community a healthier place. Unlike most media campaigns, it is not just a "top-down" approach, with a select group of community leaders and media representatives developing a single message to broadcast to the public. It invites and requires input from the public, young people, parents, and others involved in the various elements of community risk reduction.

You may remember the 1989 media campaign about the dangers of drug use supported by the Partnership for a Drug-Free America. It was among the most effective antidrug media campaigns ever created in terms of viewer recognition. One memorable image from the campaign was a series of television spots and print ads that showed scrambled eggs in a frying pan. The message: "This is your brain on drugs."

Media advocacy takes the concept of a successful media campaign several steps further. The goal is to educate the public not just against drug use but in favor of ways to reduce risk factors, strengthen protective factors, and create a healthier community where young people will have a better chance of growing up drug-free.

Rationale

Today the many forms of mass communications media—radio, television, newspapers, and magazines—play a major role, along with the home and the school, in defining life-styles, attitudes, and values. For better or worse, the mass media are powerful educators. They reach everywhere. In the average home, a television set is on seven hours a day. The average teenager listens to countless hours of radio every day and is exposed to at least 100,000 ads for alcoholic beverages before graduating from high school. Ninety-eight percent of American homes have television sets, compared with 88 percent that have indoor plumbing.

Some assert that the mass media are potentially harmful to public health—mainly through the advertising of alcoholic beverages and cigarettes, but also through programming that favorably depicts behaviors like smoking and alcohol drinking. Yet in recent years, many media outlets have also become allies of public health advocates. The media have great potential to promote health and well-being. The purpose of this program element is to make the most of the media's power to raise public awareness about drug and alcohol problems.

Goals and Objectives

Goals

- To alter community attitudes favorable toward alcohol and other drug use and to support those efforts that seek to reduce other risk factors identified in the community risk assessment
- To promote community bonding and aid in the establishment of clear community norms against drug use; to pro-

vide opportunities for recognition of positive behaviors, activities, and individual and community accomplishments

Objectives

- To develop a comprehensive, coordinated media campaign to support the "Communities That Care" approach
- To educate the local communications media in risk and protective factors and the social development strategy, encouraging them to develop a shared framework for their coverage of the alcohol and drug issue
- To teach media task force members how to interact effectively with, involve, and enlist the media in working with the "Communities That Care" project as partners
- To stimulate disussion among media representatives about their own coverage of and attitudes toward alcohol and other drug use

Supporting Research

The media advocacy approach described in this chapter is a significantly broader way of organizing and working with local media than has been attempted in the past. There are many precedents for health-related media efforts, however, and significant research in support of the more comprehensive approach advocated here.

According to one study (Black, 1989), the Partnership for a Drug-Free America campaign played a primary role in a marked shift in attitudes toward drugs among youth and college students between 1987 and 1989. The study found that in areas of high media exposure during the years of intensive use of Partnership-sponsored public service announcements, the changes in attitude were substantially greater and less favorable toward drugs than in other cities where there was no media blitz. Between 1988 and 1989, in areas of high media exposure, marijuana use declined 33 percent and cocaine use declined 15 percent. In areas of little or no exposure to Partnership messages, the declines were 15 percent and 2 percent, respectively. While these differences may reflect other community factors, they are consistent with the view that the media can play an important role in shaping community norms. Two other noteworthy mass media health promotion campaigns:

- *The Stanford Heart Disease Prevention Program and the Minnesota Heart Health Project.* Both of these programs incorporated intensive use of local media as a way to raise public awareness about how to control risk factors contributing to heart disease. Both campaigns combined mass media messages with follow-up personal communication in the form of local workshops, classes, and clinics. In both campaigns, the combination of media messages, follow-up activities, and grassroots publicity (fliers, brochures, posters) resulted in significant weight reduction, reduced cigarette smoking, and improved cholesterol and blood pressure levels in the targeted communities (Farquhar, 1985; Farquhar et al., 1984).
- *The Midwestern Prevention Project (Project STAR).* This is a communitywide drug abuse prevention project in Kansas City (Pentz, Dwyer, et al., 1989). In addition to a school-based drug education course that involved parents as well as students, the project included intensive use of local media in an informational role. The result was a broad decrease in initiation of alcohol, tobacco, and marijuana use among students in grades seven and eight.

A major study of mass media campaigns to prevent preteen and adolescent substance abuse (Winsten & DeJong, 1989) concluded that successful media campaigns have numerous elements in common. These include:
- A long-term perspective (short-term campaigns are less likely to be successful, whereas campaigns lasting a year or more have a greater likelihood of success)
- Specific efforts to address issues of broad public concern and carefully test media messages before widespread distribution
- Clearly identified target audiences
- Messages that build on the audience's current level of knowledge

- A media plan that guarantees the target audience's exposure to the campaign
- Extensive use of research

Media advocacy in the "Communities That Care" approach builds on current knowledge about the role of mass media in public health campaigns. One conclusion is that media alone do not create lasting changes in behavior. The use of media is most likely to be successful when it is part of a campaign that combines multiple outreach strategies—for example, mass media in combination with more personal approaches such as grassroots organizing and the direct involvement of health care and human service professionals, educators, and volunteers.

The campaign must emphasize local problems and needs in addition to regional or national issues. In the early stages of the campaign, there must be a media "blitz" to get the community's attention. The campaign must continue for the duration of the project, and interest must be maintained by changing the focus of the campaign from time to time—once a quarter, for example.

In short, the mass media in your community can and should be considered a valuable partner of the community board. The media are shapers of opinions and ideas; they play a key role in defining the community's values. They can help to make your community a place where illegal drug use is not tolerated, and where efforts to counter risk factors by strengthening protective factors against alcohol and other drug abuse are widely understood and supported.

Program Description

The drug story can easily, and probably will, return again and again to national media news. But it is unlikely that the level of media intensity reached in 1986 will return unless . . . a more coordinated and massive attack than has yet appeared is mounted by both public and private groups. Too often in recent years, the drug problem has been treated symbolically by national leaders. The cynicism associated with exploiting issues in this way is communicated quickly to the working press. As a consequence, coverage of the drug issue has been sometimes thoughtful, sometimes superficial [Merriam, 1989, p. 8].

Occasionally a major drug-related story hits the news and the country becomes galvanized around the drug issue. A noteworthy example was the 1986 death of basketball star Len Bias from cocaine use. Increasingly, however, single-focused, "one-shot" drug abuse prevention efforts are recognized as an inadequate response to a complex problem. Similarly, a single-message media campaign like "We say 'no' to drugs" is not enough. A more productive approach is to regard the media as a key building block in a broad, comprehensive, communitywide prevention strategy. The community as a whole needs to be educated about ways to deal with and prevent drug abuse. Community leaders, the media, and the general public should all be targeted.

To accomplish this, the media task force must learn strategies to educate the media about the importance of risk factors and the social development strategy. The task force should begin by assessing the community's media environment and becoming well informed about ways to work with the media. Task force members must learn specific skills for working as advocates for the basic concepts underlying the program and each of the other program elements the community board chooses to implement. Task force members should develop a plan for mobilizing the media to support the "Communities That Care" approach of risk reduction. Substantively, the plan should:

- Support the message that drug use is harmful.
- Communicate the values and standards of the community.
- Provide general information about issues, problems, and solutions, centering on how risk can be reduced by enhancing protective factors (presented in easy-to-understand terms).

- Create support for community board plans and lend credibility to the process.
- Increase the demand for action, thereby stimulating allocation of resources for risk reduction.
- Recognize people and prevention programs that have been effective in the community.
- Offer examples of positive behaviors and role models.

Television, radio, newspapers, and magazines have differing strengths. Television offers the widest potential audience, and its visual element makes emotional appeals possible. Television provides a variety of formats for getting the message across: public service announcements ("spots"), news and interview shows, features. It is the best medium for reaching high-risk audiences.

Radio allows for more audience targeting because programs and even whole stations have specific audiences. Although radio reaches a smaller audience than television, it may reach people who will not receive the information any other way. Teens listen to the radio, and so it provides a good medium for reaching them. Radio is inexpensive, compared with television.

The print media can convey messages in more depth than the broadcast media are able to do, although they have a relatively small audience compared with radio and television. Newspapers have the largest audience, although newspaper information has a short life compared with that of other publications. Magazine audiences are more narrowly targeted than newspaper audiences, but readers are more likely to reread or clip articles. Here are some tips on planning a media campaign.

- Develop a long-term strategic plan that divides the campaign into distinct phases, each with realistic, specific, and measurable objectives whose achievement will directly facilitate or otherwise set the stage for behavior change
- Use qualitative research methods to develop a rich understanding of potential target audiences and to inform decisions about which audiences to target
- Develop campaigns that increase public awareness of chronic

substance abuse in the society and promote debate on public policy options

- Target parents and promote parent involvement in prevention efforts
- Address target audience beliefs that impede adoption of the
  desired behavior change
- Communicate incentives for adopting the desired behavior
  change that build on the motives, needs, and values of the
  target group
- Explore the use of "image" or "life-style" advertising to promote an active, healthful life-style that excludes substance use
- Select media according to the target audience's preferences
  and the objectives of the campaign, paying greater attention to the use of radio in reaching teen audiences (adapted
  from Winsten and DeJong, 1989).

Implementation

There are almost as many ways to implement a media campaign as there are communities. Each community has its own
unique characteristics, needs, and history of media involvement
in community service. Nevertheless, a few basic principles apply to all communities undertaking a "Communities That Care"
effort.

Establishing a Media Task Force

Assigning responsibility for media efforts is a necessary first step.
People who take on this role should be well organized, articu-
late, energetic, creative, outgoing, and able to handle deadlines
and work under pressure. They should want to stay involved
in what is likely to be a long-term effort. These people should
know the community, represent its diverse elements, and have
good writing or group presentation skills.

Selecting the Media

Two distinctly different approaches to media mobilization can
be used: (1) "multiple outlet" — a total media effort using all avail-

able resources, for example, the entire range of television stations, radio stations, newspapers, and other media available in the community; or (2) "single outlet" — use of one or two media outlets only. Deciding which approach to take will be the most important step in implementing this program element. Either one may be appropriate for your community.

A multiple-outlet campaign involves attempting to blanket the community with information using all the available television stations, radio stations, newspapers, and other media. In addition to the standard outlets — newspapers, radio, and television — it might involve billboards, bus cards, community newspapers, specialty publications, fliers in laundromats, and any other available media. A consequence of the multiple-outlet approach is that no one media outlet is likely to devote an unusual amount of time or space to the campaign. And it would be advisable to have representatives of major media outlets included on the media subcommittee; otherwise, the campaign probably will not become a high priority for any of the media.

A good example of a multiple-outlet campaign took place in Oregon throughout 1988 and 1989 (Didier, 1990). The statewide campaign was conducted to recruit 400 trainers and 10,000 participants for a series of workshops using the five-session parent training program *Preparing for the Drug (Free) Years.* The campaign was supported by the highly visible leadership of Governor Neil Goldschmidt and extensive grassroots publicity efforts. The Oregon Association of Broadcasters and the Oregon Newspaper Publishers Association joined forces with several leading state agencies concerned with the well-being of youth to provide leadership in spreading the word about the campaign.

A key to the Oregon campaign's success was a variety of media materials, news releases, and television spots developed on a pro bono basis by a leading public relations firm. To kick off the campaign, the firm hosted a brunch for representatives of all the state's major media outlets at which the governor personally requested media support. To handle large numbers of responses to the media spots requesting parent volunteers, toll-free numbers with voice mail were used.

Oregon's campaign provided training to 10,000 parents in less than one year, with significant positive changes in knowledge and attitudes for those participating in the program. Up to 80 percent of participants reported they were holding family meetings after the first training session.

A single-outlet campaign involves one or two noncompetitive media partners who take on much more responsibility for the campaign than in the multiple-outlet approach. The partner(s) make a commitment of significant time and resources to the campaign, and the campaign becomes closely identified with the particular medium involved. This approach might include a leading newspaper and television station, for example, and the campaign would be identified as "their" campaign in close conjunction with the community board. Representatives from each of these outlets should be included as members of the media subcommittee and perhaps on the community board as well.

A two-year single-outlet media campaign focusing on prenatal care was successfully initiated through a partnership between the Utah Department of Health and a major television station, KUTV, in Salt Lake City (1987–1989). "Baby Your Baby" was supported by a broad coalition of public and private organizations and centered on a $2.25 million campaign comprised of four six-month "waves" of intensive television coverage. Each wave advanced the main theme of informing prospective mothers about effective prenatal care.

The television station, as a major "Baby Your Baby" sponsor, produced the main elements: a series of television public service announcements, two half-hour television documentaries, regular spots promoting available services, and frequent segments on local programs, including *PM Magazine,* the news, and live public affairs call-in shows. Other media approaches initiated by the campaign task force included ads in newspapers and *TV Guide,* statewide radio spots, viewer guides, posters, and bus cards. Community outreach activities included coupon books requiring physician validation; information cards for health care providers; pamphlets distributed through hospitals, clinics, and direct mailings; hand delivery of information during the March of Dimes Mothers' March; newborn newsletters to new mothers; and booths at relevant statewide conferences.

Initial results for the Utah campaign indicated it was

directly responsible for a variety of improvements in the delivery of prenatal care in Utah: 60 percent of Medicaid mothers who sought prenatal treatment in 1988 mentioned the campaign as the reason they sought treatment; the number of mothers who sought prenatal care in Department of Health clinics nearly doubled in the first year of the campaign; and at the end of the first year of the campaign, the infant death rate in Utah had dropped 8 percent.

Both approaches — multiple-outlet and single-outlet — can be effective, depending on the community. Here are some questions to ask in considering the two alternatives:

- What is the size of the community? How many television stations, radio stations, newspapers, and other media are actually in the community? The larger the community, the more media outlets it is likely to have. A total media effort is more appropriate for a smaller community. In a larger community, it may make more sense to work with just a few outlets.
- Are the media in the community highly competitive, or do they cooperate in community service efforts?
- Are any particular media currently interested in the issue or already covering it? Which media outlets are sympathetic to issues associated with youth and drug abuse?
- Have the media undertaken major community service projects in the past? If so, what did they look like? How were they organized? Were they multiple- or single-outlet campaigns?
- How involved is the top management of the local media outlets in community activities and issues?
- How strong is the advertising climate in the community? Communications media may not be as inclined to get heavily involved in a community campaign if revenues are weak. Financial sponsorship may need to be identified early in the planning phase.
- A related issue: How much money is spent on beer and wine advertising in the community? In communities with major sports teams, beer advertising is an important source of

revenue for local media, and a challenge to that revenue may have an impact on your media relationships. Your task force will need to discuss this.

- What might be the result for service providers in the community of a major media blitz? Would local agencies be prepared to handle the additional requests that might result?

Another important consideration is the specific audience to target. This will vary from one community to another and will depend on the elements the community board chooses for the overall program of risk reduction. The approach for encouraging parents to participate in parent training for drug abuse prevention, for example, would be very different from an effort to publicize changes in community policies to restrict the availability of alcohol for teens.

Approaching the Media

Once your media task force has decided on a specific approach (single- or multiple-outlet), training should be sought to prepare task force members to work with the media. The Training and Technical Assistance section of this chapter offers a list of specific skills that should be covered by training. In general, it will be important for those contacting decision makers in local media organizations to have some familiarity with the language and perspective of each medium, to be clear about media task force goals, and to emphasize that this campaign is different from conventional public service campaigns. This underscores the long-term nature of the "Communities That Care" approach.

In presenting your plans to media representatives, the emphasis should be on both practical and ethical reasons for their involvement. Since they are corporate citizens of the community, these problems are theirs, too, and they have a particular obligation to the public to provide a forum for discussion of community problems. It also makes good business sense for them to be involved. The community board can be an important source of ideas and issues. Outreach activities on the part of the media can increase their visibility and enhance goodwill—

television stations that are perceived as being more involved in their communities are generally number 1 or are on their way to being number 1. That means higher ratings and higher revenues.

Selecting an Advertising Agency

An advertising agency can be helpful in developing a variety of materials such as a logo, television spots, print materials, graphics, and other key elements of the campaign. If possible, find an agency willing to work with the campaign on a pro bono basis. Although the members of the task force do not need to be experts in advertising and design themselves, they should have a clear idea about the type of campaign they have in mind. This will require a study of similar campaigns, television spots, brochures, fliers, and related materials. Other important considerations in selecting an advertising agency include the following:

- Has the agency done similar types of campaigns before? What is that agency's experience with health-related campaigns? With working with local groups and volunteers?
- What do the task force members think about the quality of the agency's work?
- What media strategies does the task force have in mind (for example, television spots, newspaper advertisements, and so on)? Are those consistent with the agency's area of expertise?
- Can the agency provide the services you need? These might include creative strategy development, market research, tailoring messages to target audience characteristics of age or culture, production of materials, help with planning message distribution, placement of media spots, and design of community events.

Distinguishing Between Advertising and Programming

The media task force will need to become well informed about the different types of approaches that can be used in a media campaign, especially the distinction between advertising and programming. One aspect of the campaign, for example, might be a "blitz" of pro bono messages throughout the community in a variety of media (public service advertising). This approach facilitates communication of a single, consistent message through a variety of media—for instance, television and radio spots, billboards, bus cards, and so on—which can raise awareness about a specific topic or issue. Media organizations ordinarily donate the air time for these messages, and they may also donate production and staff.

A well-planned and well-coordinated public service effort can play an important role in getting your message across to a broad audience (Hawkins, Catalano, & Kent, 1991). Media organizations are flooded every month with announcements and information about worthy causes. The ones they print or air in the free time they allocate for public service announcements are likely to be those that are the most clearly focused and professionally produced.

Programming is an entirely different way of getting your message across. It might consist of the following:

- News stories or features
- Interviews on radio or television talk shows, public affairs programs, or "magazine" shows
- Articles in local newspapers, in columns, or in special sections
- Telethons, fundraisers, and special events
- Broadcasts focused on the special needs of the various program elements
- Documentaries
- Letters to the editor, editorials, and replies
- Community calendars and bulletin boards

To provide local media with interesting stories, it can be helpful to develop a list of who's who in alcohol and drug abuse and related fields in your community—people involved in prevention and risk reduction who are prepared and willing to be interviewed by the local media and who can present information about your community mobilization and risk reduction efforts clearly and articulately.

Training and Technical Assistance

Training and technical assistance for this element should (1) help members of the media task force become well informed and skillful media advocates — able to work collegially with local media representatives and knowledgeable about ways to convey a variety of messages related to the project, and (2) give task force members the tools to educate media about risk-focused drug abuse prevention approaches consistent with the social development strategy.

Training should be highly interactive and participatory, including specific "how-to" information and practice. Media task force members will need to know how to present the concepts of risk and protective factors to the media. They will be responsible for designing and developing the media campaign — including themes, focus, and elements — and they must determine whether a single- or multiple-outlet approach will be best. They need to know how to approach the media, make their activities newsworthy, arrange for advertising supplements in local newspapers, write effective news releases and fact sheets, and make the best use of local celebrities.

Technical assistance throughout the media project is advisable in, for example, selecting the most effective media approaches for each element, critiquing news releases, and developing videotapes. The goal of technical assistance should be to develop capacity in the task force to carry out media projects competently and effectively.

The antidrug messages developed by the Partnership for a Drug-Free America may be used as part of a community's overall media strategy. Permission to use these materials may be obtained through the Partnership.

Evaluation

Process Evaluation

Specific ways to assess the delivery of media campaigns and the responses they generate may include the following:

- Tracking the number of phone calls to a local number for information or help
- Tracking the number of requests for information
- Using a clipping service to track coverage of events and programs developed in conjunction with campaigns
- Obtaining logs of radio and television public service announcements aired, including the times of day they were aired and the value of the air time correlated to calls to hotlines, attendance at events, and so on
- Getting ratings for broadcast programs
- Compiling totals on the distribution of materials offered in conjunction with campaigns
- Counting attendance at workshops or other public events advertised or promoted in the media

Outcome Evaluation

Also important to assess will be changes in knowledge, attitudes, and behaviors resulting from media campaigns. Community members may be surveyed about their knowledge, attitudes, and use of drugs. Risk and protective risk factors addressed by the media campaign may be reassessed to evaluate change.

Resources

The federal Office for Substance Abuse Prevention provides training on media campaign development tailored to local community needs. Information on training programs may be obtained by contacting:

Robert Denniston, Director
Division of Community Programs
Office for Substance Abuse Prevention
5600 Fishers Lane, Rockwall II, Rm. 9C03
Rockville, MD 20857
(301) 443-0373

Antidrug messages for all media are available free of charge to be used by local community groups as long as they are not supporting commercial interests. Community groups may tailor some of these materials for local purposes, with approval of the Partnership. For information about available messages and other programs of the Partnership, contact:

The Partnership for a Drug-Free America
666 Third Avenue
New York, NY 10017
(212) 922-1560

Part Three

SUPPORTING COMMUNITY PREVENTION PROGRAMS

A. Baron Holmes IV　　　　　　　　*Chapter 13*
Gary D. Gottfredson
Janet Y. Miller

Resources and Strategies
for Funding

As communities consider mobilizing to prevent adolescent alcohol and other drug abuse, they will inevitably confront the
question "Where will we get the money?" Escalating demands
on health and human services during the 1980s show no sign
of letting up in the 1990s. Service planners are recognizing that
new ways of looking at programming and new strategies for
funding will be required to reduce the problems we face.

The previous chapters have shown that community mobilization to prevent problems of drug and alcohol abuse requires
changes that affect many groups and organizations and extend
over time. We are not talking about a simple "quick-fix" but
a diversified, long-term investment. No single funding source
will support all the programs initiated by task forces using the
"Communities That Care" approach; no single provider or system will supply the services.

The recognition that resources for community change will
come from a variety of sources and take many forms comes at
a time when education and human service organizations are

struggling to cope with intensive new demands. With slower growth in federal spending, new programs must look beyond the *Federal Register,* new state appropriations, or foundation grant guidelines. Although these resources can be important sources of start-up funding, the most significant bases for ongoing support of community risk reduction will be the existing institutions and systems of the community. The first question a community board should ask about funding is "Where is the money for children and families currently being spent?" The answer will identify the institutions and systems that control the resources required for new programs and that contain the capacity for restructuring programs toward the goal of risk reduction.

Where Is the Money Now?

Community boards should answer this question: Where are health, education, and human service dollars currently being spent? More specifically, what is the proportion of funding allocated to child, youth, and family programs in health, mental health, welfare, corrections, and education budgets? Although this information is obtainable, few local, state, or even federal government agencies are organized to make it readily accessible. If the information cannot be easily compiled, community boards should recruit a state or local government budget expert to help identify current local spending patterns.

    Spending figures for two states and for the federal government serve to illustrate the value of this analysis. This is a broadbrush analysis; community boards will want to look in greater depth at their own local funding picture. Our first example is South Carolina, where analysis revealed that five of every six dollars spent on children and youth were spent in the schools (Figure 13.1). The remaining one dollar covered all other programs, including health, economic support, treatment, and prevention — an amount equivalent to the cost of transporting children from home to school and back over the school year.

    In Washington state, for the 1991–93 biennium, 88.7 percent of all spending for children, youth, and families was allocated to K-12 education (Figure 13.2). During this two-year

Figure 13.1. State of South Carolina:
1989 Spending for Children and Youth.

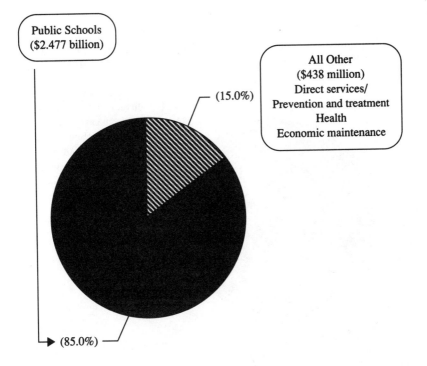

Public Schools
($2.477 billion)

All Other
($438 million)
Direct services/
Prevention and treatment
Health
Economic maintenance

(15.0%)

(85.0%)

period, all spending for children and youth services in the state's social and health agencies totaled $899,300,000, compared with $7,085,000,000 in the schools.

On the federal level, of the $36 billion dollars spent on children (excluding entitlement funds), $15 billion (almost 42 percent) goes to education. The remaining $21 billion is divided among all other programs for children and youth.

Although funding patterns and proportions vary from state to state, it is safe to predict that in all states, the largest share of spending for children and youth is tied to schools. Because such a large share of existing resources is absorbed by education, it is clear that community boards must enlist the active participation of school leaders and educational institutions in the comprehensive risk reduction effort. Moreover, the regularity

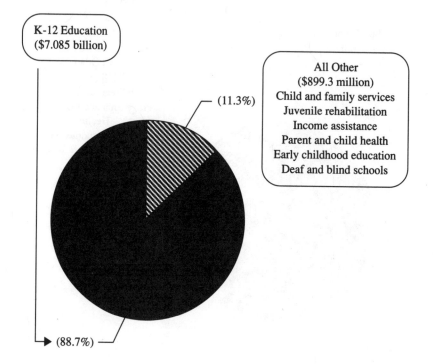

Figure 13.2. State of Washington:
1991–93 Spending for Children, Youth, and Families.

and relative intensity of contact between school personnel and children underscores the school's significance as an institution of key importance in risk reduction programs for children.

New initiatives must be grounded within these institutions, or at least connected to them. The extensiveness and strength of existing systems can provide economies of scale and a stable institutional infrastructure for service provision. Building new programs independent of these established systems risks marginalizing these programs.

Beyond economic reality, schools have uniquely broad access to and credibility with children and families. This makes the argument for involving schools even more compelling. The schools are, more than any other institution, embedded in the community; they have the children; they have a degree of access to parents; and they need to reduce school-related risk factors for drug and alcohol abuse in order to do their job. To a lesser degree, the same considerations dictate building our risk reduction efforts into other established child-serving programs such as health clinics, community youth centers, and so on.

School personnel may question our emphasis on schools as central in risk reduction strategies, pointing to the increasing demands placed on them to meet needs of children that extend far beyond the traditional education role. We are not suggesting that schools take on this task alone, but that prevention programs work as partners with schools to increase effectiveness and efficiency. In some cases, this may involve liaisons between schools and other services, as when parent trainers leading workshops on "How to Help Your Child Succeed in School" connect with teachers to make parent homework assignments relevant to what teachers are teaching (see Chapter Eight). In other cases, it may mean that prevention programs — Head Start or other early childhood education programs — are housed within elementary schools (see Chapter Seven). In still other cases, it may mean that teaching approaches and curricula are adapted to incorporate risk reduction strategies (see Chapters Nine and Ten) or that school management and drug and alcohol policies are developed around principles that ensure a positive and productive climate for learning (see Chapters Nine and Twelve). Far from imposing additional burdens on school administrators and teachers, changes like these will free them to focus on their jobs as educators.

Advocates for grassroots change may also object to our focus on schools, but for different reasons. They may point to the failure of institutionalized systems to respond flexibly and creatively to needs. In many communities, a strong momentum favoring community-based programs has emerged; it is characterized by vitality, openness, and creative ideas too often missing in bureaucratic systems. The reality is that both grassroots groups and established systems can gain by cooperating in risk reduction. Community-based programs need the stability and reach of large institutions; large institutions need the empowering vision and grassroots ties of community programs.

Creative Funding Approaches
for Resource-Poor Communities

When a community board has identified where the money is currently being spent, prospects for new program support should begin to emerge. For example, within a school district, certain categorical program funding is usually available for students with particular needs. Use of these funds may be flexible; often funds that are available are not being used to the extent allowable to support programs that enhance schools as protective environments for social development. The following examples illustrate ways that available resources can be put to use in funding prevention efforts.

Chapter 1 Funds

The largest federal educational initiative intended to benefit low-income students and the schools that serve them is "Chapter 1." If disadvantaged students are to succeed early in school and thereby avoid the failure that promotes adolescent risk-taking behavior, then Chapter 1 funds must become a powerful vehicle for effective early education.

Until recently, the Chapter 1 law and regulations required that money be spent on remediation of basic skill deficiencies of identified low achievers in schools with a high percentage of low-income, disadvantaged students. Schools with Chapter 1 money have traditionally developed a mixture of self-contained, pull-out, and in-class programs for pupils identified as needing remedial assistance. Dissatisfaction with these models is widespread. Revisions made in 1988 to the federal legislation governing the Chapter 1 program have created the opportunity for major changes across the country that can make Chapter 1 an effective vehicle for funding many elements of the "Communities That Care" strategy.

One of these changes allows school systems to develop "schoolwide" programs in schools with a large percentage of low-income students. The main requirement for such programs is that they be reasonably expected to produce substantial educational improvement. They present an opportunity to redirect funds traditionally spent on pull-out programs, self-contained classes, and resource teachers to support schoolwide programs with promise for risk reduction. Communities considering implementation of the school development and management or instructional improvements elements described earlier in this book should consider funding these approaches through Chapter 1.

Job Training Partnership Act

The Job Training Partnership Act (JTPA) is designed as a community-based, private sector–oriented program with potential for ameliorating risk for adolescent problem behavior. JTPA has several positive features. It is an employment and training program that aims to enhance economic opportunity for disadvantaged youths. If provided at the appropriate point in young people's development, such employment and training can encourage bonding to work and inhibit negative or unhealthful risk-taking behaviors. Organizationally, the private sector provides leadership through locally based private industry councils, which promote private initiatives for training and employing young people. JTPA presents an opportunity for multiprogram funding coalitions through Title II-B, the Summer Youth Employment and Training Program. Title II-B offers not only summer employment but also a broad range of training and development possibilities.

An example of the multidimensional programming possible through Title II-B is Public/Private Ventures' Summer Training and Education Program (STEP), which seeks to keep dropout-prone fourteen- and fifteen-year-olds in school by operating a multipart program over two summers and one intervening school year. Each summer, STEP provides ninety hours of group and individually paced instruction in reading and math, at least eighty hours of part-time summer employment, and eighteen hours of instruction in life skills and decision making, including topics on AIDS risks, sexual activity, and substance abuse. During the school year, the program provides counseling and case management, individually and in groups. The extra cost for STEP services beyond summer employment is approximately $460 per participant each summer and $310 for the school-year component.

This is an approach to funding that can support many of the program elements included in "Communities That Care." In communities serving JTPA-eligible youth, community boards might use this mechanism for the social competence promotion curricula and instructional improvements elements of the strategy (Chapters Ten and Eleven).

Family Support Act

The Family Support Act (FSA) is the major piece of federal welfare reform legislation passed in 1988. The emphasis on limiting welfare dependence through employment was expanded to include the provision of education and other services necessary for economic independence for welfare recipients. Among other things, the FSA now often ties AFDC payments to participation in schooling, encourages programs focusing on teen and young adult single mothers, provides that sufficient funds be spent for day care, and provides a substantial federal match for state funds spent on a variety of services to AFDC families. The FSA opens up major possibilities for program development.

The FSA offers potential for reducing dependence on welfare and its attendant problems. It can be a challenge, however, to structure local responses. At present, welfare service providers and educational services nationwide are isolated from each other. The FSA offers opportunities for sharing the burden of preventive education. Sharing would not only help to integrate the currently fragmented activities for children from high-risk families, but it would also multiply existing resources by taking advantage of federal matching funds.

Programs that can be funded by welfare agencies include adult education, parent education, tutoring and counseling for AFDC children, and a variety of other prevention activities. Programs such as these could be sited in schools serving large proportions of AFDC children. Several program elements included in "Communities That Care" could fit within the parameters of FSA funding, including parent education components of prenatal, early infancy, and early childhood programs (Chapters Six and Seven) and parent training programs (Chapter Eight).

Curriculum Enhancement

Several programs directed at preventing adolescent problem behavior can be implemented within existing public school budgets at a relatively low cost. School improvements (see Chapters Nine through Eleven) often involve changes in instructional practices or content that can be carried out by personnel already employed. For example, a health education curriculum emphasizing the skills needed to resist undesirable peer influences can be incorporated into general course offerings at little or no extra cost beyond that of curriculum and inservice training for teachers. Similarly, teachers can be trained in improved methods of classroom management and instruction described in Chapter Ten. Many interventions require primarily a one-time expense of curriculum selection and staff training.

Parent, Business, and Community Support

The rationale for partnerships between public agencies and private groups is compelling. Private initiative and support not only supplement public expenditures; they offer the possibility for prevention programming that is impossible through public programs alone. Families and schools are the two social institutions with the most extensive and intensive contact with young people. Parents are so central to child development that it is hard to comprehend why school and human service programs so often ignore them. Employers and churches are primary organizational contacts with adults, many of whom are parents. These groups must become partners in prevention and program development. This will happen only if efficient and effective techniques of collaboration are applied.

Until recently, the design, testing, and evaluation of these partnerships received scant emphasis. When resources were growing, attention focused on building governmental capacity. Public policy concentrated on the direct provision of services. Today, resource growth has slowed, making it necessary to create innovative public-private mechanisms for prevention. Developing partnerships requires careful planning, adequate staffing, effective management, and ongoing evaluation. Such development demands investment, yet it offers a wide range of potentially high-yield benefits that compare favorably with existing services when the goal is reducing risk by enhancing protection against delinquency and drug abuse.

Health Insurance Reimbursement

Another funding possibility is the use of Medicaid and third-party insurance programs. How many school systems employ school nurses to do health and mental health screening for low-income children and bill Medicaid for these services? How many schools located near military bases have made attempts to integrate prevention programming with military-base health services? School-based health clinics using insurance and other health funds should become an important vehicle for prevention services. These clinics could offer parent training in prevention strategies, as well as training in social competence and peer resistance for students, as described in Chapters Eight and Eleven.

Making Programs Financially Stable

Regardless of the source of funding, the programs that will survive are the ones designed and implemented to be responsive to the needs of the community and accountable to policy makers. Most demonstration programs and new initiatives cease to operate within a year or two after the initial funding has ended. They fail to become institutionalized—that is, they fail to become integrated into the organizational and community landscape. In the next section of this chapter, we will outline what it takes to make a program stable. But we first describe the primary reasons that new projects so often fail to become institutionalized.

We can all think of projects that have disappeared after the demonstration grant ended. They usually start with high hopes and great fanfare: a press release, media coverage, the appointment of an enthusiastic project director, the creation of a planning committee. High expectations accompany the infusion of new outside funding in the form of a federal, foundation, or state grant, usually limited in time from one to five years. The purpose of the project is almost always innovative, a change from the status quo.

Grant writers envisioning the project rarely look beyond the life of the grant to plan for permanence. At best, other organizations in the community are asked to send letters of support for the proposal, letters that often reveal little or no understanding or commitment to support the project once the grant runs out. Organization executives and budget officials are overwhelmed with requests and have a long line of priority "pet" causes waiting for funding. This is the scenario that so often leads to the failure even of effective demonstration projects, keeping them from becoming stable features of the community. Demonstration programs and new initiatives fail for the following reasons:

- Providers or administrators of existing programs reject the innovation that was promoted by "outsiders."
- Decision makers who control the resources do not feel that the innovation deserves to be a funding priority.
- The public does not support the innovation and does not pressure decision makers to allocate resources for it.
- The innovation creates an expensive "add-on" program.
- Costs per client are high, but the innovation's effects are modest or negligible.
- Decision makers are not convinced of the innovation's effectiveness.
- High program costs are borne entirely by demonstration funding, rather than by incorporating private or existing resources.

The three organizing concepts *acceptability, budgetability,* and *cost-effectiveness* are helpful in planning for long-term funding for new programs. Acceptable, budgetable, and cost-effective programs can be institutionalized. An acceptable program is one that clients, providers, funders, key constituencies, and the public want. Because they want it, they will work to support it. A budgetable program is one that can be paid for with resources that are available — or that can be made available in the foreseeable future. A cost-effective program is one that provides a good return on public investment. All things considered, it is a prudent investment because it reduces social problems noticeably in relation to dollars expended.

These principles are important to the "Communities That Care" strategy because the program elements seek to prevent a wide range of serious problems that threaten large numbers of young people: alcohol and drug abuse, delinquency, teen pregnancy, school dropout, unemployment, and social dependency. We cannot afford the loss of youngsters to these social and health problems or the cost of expensive treatment and aftercare programs.

Despite the recent availability of funds for prevention of alcohol and other drug problems through the Department of Justice, the National Institute on Drug Abuse (NIDA), the Office for Substance Abuse Prevention (OSAP), and the U.S. Department of Education, it is unlikely that significant long-term increases in funding can be expected from federal sources in the near future. Federal funds may be available for demonstration projects, but for long-term program institutionalization, communities must reprogram existing resources. New programs must be built in collaboration with schools, parents, churches, employers, criminal justice, and existing social and health service programs.

Acceptability

Given the importance of state and local funding sources, acceptability must be established with state and local government officials who set the human services agenda through legislation and policy. One of the most important determinants of a program's acceptability is its grassroots program reputation — the perceptions of the program by clients, voters, service providers, the local media, and local political leaders.

For clients, this perception will rest on how well the program meets their needs, on whether they feel they are treated with dignity by service providers, and on their personal costs in terms of time, money, inconvenience, or stigma. Providers' perceptions of the program's efficacy and importance to participants will be a major factor in judging its acceptability. The program's acceptability to providers may depend, in part, on how the program affects valued roles and financial security, or on how burdensome the regulations, demands for documentation, and paperwork seem, and this should be recognized.

State agency personnel and administrators are likely to assess acceptability by considering statewide program experience, national research, what other states are doing, their perceptions of other possible uses of the money, and their views of the wishes of political leaders in the state. Legislative staff may consider evaluation studies, reports about program operations, and perceived alternative uses of the required money. Finally, legislators will be influenced by the media, lobbyists, constituent opinion, and pressures to use money for other purposes.

All of these people—clients, providers, local decision makers, state agency personnel, and legislative staff and legislators—are constituencies who can help to institutionalize a program if they perceive it to be needed and acceptable. Constituencies grow out of public, provider, media, and legislator consensus on needs to be addressed. A consensus is now emerging on the need to ameliorate the personal, social, and economic costs of adolescent problem behaviors—drug and alcohol abuse, delinquency, pregnancy, and school dropout—all of which emerge from shared risk factors. These problems can be prevented by addressing these shared risk factors while enhancing protective factors against the problems.

"Communities That Care" can help build a constituency for prevention programs. It provides a research-based, developmental framework for understanding and addressing adolescent problems and a process for community mobilization to reduce risk factors and enhance protective factors. Diverse groups concerned with crime reduction, family welfare, child health, preschool programs, and the school success of elementary and middle school students all share concerns about the common risk factors for adolescent health and behavior problems and can become a constituency of allies, joining together to prevent the severe adolescent problems capturing headlines.

In addition, acceptability can be increased by providing comparisons of the costs of prevention programs with the far greater costs of treatment, incarceration, and other interventions for drug-abusing and delinquent youth. Such comparisons are powerful tools for constituency building.

The "Communities That Care" strategy incorporates these principles of acceptability by starting with involvement of local community leaders, by building on a theoretically sound risk and resource assessment, and by developing program innovations that have a sound basis in research.

Budgetability

A first principle for developing budgetable programs is that their funding must be within the limits of the choices of state and local decision makers. Increases in most program areas (such as health or education) are likely to remain stable within a range around their historical budget shares. Any growth will likely come from real dollar growth of state and local resources. Historical budget shares or allocations for different types of governmental services are fairly stable because the political pressure groups that created the shares change slowly. Consequently, a budgetable program will usually embody relatively modest increases in per-person program costs.

A second principle is that budgetable programs reduce the need for large new appropriations by entering into collaborative, multiprogram funding coalitions. Such collaborative programming pools and focuses scattered resources and, by concentrating the resources of several agencies, helps to resolve the dilemma of resource requirements that diverge from historical patterns.

A third principle for developing budgetable programs is to use currently appropriated dollars more effectively to improve programs. Program improvements make better use of existing resources (money, people, buildings) than do current practices. This principle means that new programs should be organized within existing regular activities of organizations or agencies from the outset, or that plans should be made for demonstrations to be integrated with those activities over time. Most of the elements selected for the "Communities That Care" strategy can be integrated with existing programs and services. They are consistent with the goals of many federal, state, and local funding initiatives and can thus be incorporated within current budgets.

Cost-Effectiveness

By far the greatest potential for institutionalizing prevention programs lies in leveraging base funding for greater productivity — that is, getting more program benefit from dollars already being spent. Some excellent strategies for cost-effectiveness include targeting services toward the clients most likely to need them, creating broad environmental changes that influence the behavior of many people at a low per-person cost, integrating programs, and identifying through evaluation no-yield and low-yield programs whose resources can be rechanneled to more productive uses.

For a prevention program, effectiveness is measured by reduction or elimination of risk factors for the problems to be prevented. Program and policy developers must assess both the target problems (such as drug and alcohol abuse, delinquency, or pregnancy) and the risk factors for those problems. A parenting education program for families with young children, for example, will require many years before any discernible effect on adolescent problem behavior of the children is revealed. But such a program should be able to demonstrate early evidence of effectiveness in ameliorating risk factors such as poor family management practices, child misconduct, and academic failure.

These early risk factors must be explained and evaluated

with guidance from a clearly articulated prevention theory. The social development strategy provides a basis for deciding which activities are important and which are irrelevant or peripheral. It also helps in explaining to constituencies and decision makers why diverse elements of a community prevention program are affordable, acceptable, and cost-effective.

A second consideration in determining cost-effectiveness is that prevention program effects should not be measured by a single outcome, but by a wide range of potential benefits and costs. Genuinely successful primary prevention programs are likely to involve a variety of program components that have a cumulative effect on the target population. To know the full effect of a prevention program therefore requires information about changes in the risks of a number of related negative or unhealthy outcomes.

Program implementers should seek to promote among their constituencies and decision makers a keen interest in evidence about cost-effectiveness. Thus, a third principle — generating and communicating evidence of cost-effectiveness — requires emphasis: assessment of cost-effectiveness should begin with a review of the cost-effectiveness of similar programs evaluated elsewhere. This knowledge should be made available to all relevant parties.

Cost-effectiveness of prevention programs can be increased through participation of community helpers such as volunteers and business people who share the goals and objectives of the program but whose efforts do not involve the expenditure of funds controlled by policy makers. A program that enlists the effort of "off-budget" collaborators, whether individuals or organizations, may show that effectiveness relative to program expenditures is high. A fourth principle for enhancing program cost-effectiveness: enlist the collaboration of others who share the goals of the program.

Organizing Strategies for Acceptable, Budgetable, Cost-Effective Programs

"Communities That Care" community boards can apply organizing strategies that enhance acceptability, budgetability, and cost-effectiveness. New programs are born out of a perceived need for alternatives to current ways of addressing a problem. A demonstration program is, at its heart, an attempt to show how existing practices can be changed and what the consequences of these changes will be. In this section, we suggest some strategies for changing the status quo through acceptable, budgetable, and cost-effective programs—and for maintaining the change once introduced.

Seek Opportunities for Reorganizing

Sometimes large amounts of money consumed by ongoing programs can be used in new ways. Opportunities for reorganization may occur because of dissatisfaction about current programs (for example, the failure of remedial programs to enable disadvantaged students to catch up with their peers or of child protective service and foster care programs to keep children in healthy, nurturing families). In addition, changes in rules and regulations that apply to programs may present opportunities for program reorganization, as illustrated by changes in the guidelines for two of the federal programs mentioned earlier—schoolwide Chapter 1 remedial options or the Family Support Act to help single mothers off welfare.

Employ Techniques to Unfreeze the Status Quo

Even when opportunities for reorganizing resources are available, bureaucratic systems usually resist change. One of the virtues of demonstration programs is that they are laboratories for trying new ideas. "Waivers" of policies or regulations—not permanent changes in policies or regulations—can be requested, with decisions about permanent change made later. It can also be useful to analyze laws and regulations to determine whether the status quo is an inevitable consequence of law or simply one set of options institutionalized by habit. Commonly held notions about policy, law, or regulation may be incorrect.

Use Information as a Tool

Two kinds of information are particularly useful: (1) information about how an organization's practices compare with available alternatives, and (2) information about how current outcomes compare with the desired outcomes. Be sure decision makers and practitioners understand what they are doing as compared with available alternatives. Practitioners can be expected to know what their organization does, but they often do not know what the alternatives are or what other organizations do. For example, they might not realize that the same money they spend on first-grade repeaters is used in another state for summer enrichment or tutoring to ensure that students pass the first grade.

Use information to contrast current outcomes with desired outcomes and to identify programs that are less effective than desired. For example, a school board might be surprised to learn that the 4 NCE (Normal Curve Equivalent) gain of the typical elementary reading student might be achieved cost-free by replacing tracking with a continuous regrouping system that produces homogeneous groups in reading and math.

As discussed earlier, outcome information organized as "risk indicators" can be a powerful force for change. For example, in the last decade, regular reports of test scores have been prepared on a school-by-school basis and serve as one kind of "accountability" indicator. Lower-than-acceptable test scores create great pressure for changing practices at the classroom, school building, district, and state levels. Similarly, data on the number of students over age for grade could call attention to needed interventions for increasing academic success.

Indicators should accurately reflect the desired outcomes, yet many indicator systems seem poorly designed for this purpose. For example, most educational testing programs are organized to provide scores at each grade level (for example, the percentage of eighth graders meeting a state competency standard). Unfortunately, grade-level information systems rarely provide information on what we really need to know: the proportion of thirteen-year-old children in the general population who surpass minimum criteria for eighth graders. This would take into account the repeaters, dropouts, suspended, expelled, and other nontested (for instance, special education) students at the specified age level.

Establish New Rules and Operating Procedures

Changes in rules and procedures help to institutionalize a new program. This might include such simple mechanisms as application forms, reporting requirements and forms, and standard operating procedures. Eventually, the application of these new rules and operating procedures becomes habitual. An example is a school's establishment of the practice of telephoning or sending a letter to parents of all students who are repeatedly absent, fail a course, or have a serious discipline problem, or sending a letter of congratulations to parents of all students whose grades improved from one year to another.

Use Program Funds to Work for Institutionalization

Although funds granted to establish model programs are often essential for initiating trials of prevention innovations, sometimes this kind of funding can thwart a community's capacity to institutionalize new programs by limiting acceptability, budgetability, or cost-effectiveness. Employing program managers and change agents to get a program going is usually necessary. Similarly, employing new staff may be necessary for a limited time to demonstrate that alternative practices are superior before modifying job requirements for existing staff. Generally, however, programs relying heavily on grant funds for new personnel are unlikely to be institutionalized unless a clear path to financing these costs in the future is available. Costs for training, technical assistance, and other start-up activities necessary to implement an innovation are usually productive uses of grant funds if they are designed not to be ongoing expenses.

Another fruitful use of grant funds is to invest in organization development activities, including redesigning jobs; team building and role negotiation; altering goal, incentive, or reward structures for personnel or institutions; modeling new practices for practitioners; and changing organizational structures and functions.

Similarly, it is usually productive to use grant funds to facilitate broader participation and involvement in the program.

In the "Communities That Care" approach, for instance, parents are an enormous potential resource. Other groups to consider are media, human service agencies, schools, law enforcement, religious organizations, and businesses.

Finally, grant funds for new programs should be used for evaluation to secure information about program results and cost-effectiveness. There is no reason to continue funding programs that have no significant effect.

Summary

Ten principles for acceptable, budgetable, and cost-effective programs should guide "Communities That Care" boards as they plan for stable, institutionalized programs:

1. Promote acceptability of the program at the state and local level.
2. Build constituencies by clearly communicating the program's underlying premises and theory.
3. Emphasize program improvement that better utilizes existing resources and seeks future funds within realistic resource limits.
4. Focus attention on both ultimate outcome objectives of the program and the risk factors directly addressed.
5. Demonstrate cost-effectiveness for the full range of relevant costs and benefits, not just the immediate program outcomes.
6. Use program development and evaluation methods to improve the cost-effectiveness of the program over time.
7. Work collaboratively with organizations sharing compatible goals.
8. Employ techniques to unfreeze the status quo.
9. Use information as a tool to increase decision makers' knowledge about funding alternatives.
10. Establish new rules and operating procedures so that it becomes easier to sustain the program than to revert to prior practices.

Closing Note

You can mobilize your community to protect its children against drug abuse and other health and behavior problems. By putting the "Communities That Care" strategy into operation, you can assess your community's current risks and resources. You can use the knowledge you gain to start action programs that address the risk factors prevalent in your community and enhance the protective factors of bonding and clear standards for behavior. You can work together with your community to create an environment that promotes healthy development. It is a job worth doing.

References

Ainsworth, M. D. S., Behar, M. C., Water, E., & Wall, S. (1978). *Patterns of attachment: A psychological study of the strange situation.* Hillsdale, NJ: Erlbaum.

Akers, R. L. (1977). *Deviant behavior: A social learning approach* (2nd ed.). Belmont, CA: Wadsworth.

Allen, G. J., Chinsky, J. M., Larcen, S. W., Lochman, J. E., & Selinger, J. U. (1976). *Community psychology and the schools: A behaviorally oriented multilevel preventive approach.* Hillsdale, NJ: Erlbaum.

Anisfeld, E., Casper, V., Nozyce, M., & Cunningham, N. (1990). Does infant carrying promote attachment? An experimental study of the effects of increased physical contact on the development of attachment. *Child Development, 61,* 1617–1627.

Anisfeld, E., & Pincus, M. (1987). The Post-Partum Support Project: Serving young mothers and older women through home visiting. *Zero to Three, 8*(1), 13–15.

Aronson, E., Bridgeman, D. L., & Geffner, R. (1978). Interdependent interactions and prosocial behavior. *Journal of Research and Development in Education, 12,* 16–27.

Bandura, A. (1977). Self-efficacy: Toward a unifying theory of behavioral change. *Psychological Review, 84,* 191–215.

Barnard, D. E., Booth, C. L., Mitchell, S. K., & Telzrow, R. W. (1988). Newborn nursing models: A test of early intervention to high-risk infants and families. In E. Hibbs (Ed.), *Children and families: Studies in prevention and intervention* (pp. 63–81). Madison, CT: International Universities Press.

Barnard, K. E. (1989). *Difficult life circumstances manual.* Seattle, WA: NCAST Publications.

Barnard, K. E. (1991). *Washington State Plan for Public Health Nurses.* University of Washington School of Nursing contract with Washington State Department of Health. Seattle: University of Washington.

Barnard, K. E., Hammond, M., Booth, C. L., Bee, H. L., Mitchell, S. K., & Spieker, S. J. (1989). Measurement and meaning of parent-child interaction. In F. J. Morrison, C. E. Lord, & D. P. Keating (Eds.), *Applied developmental psychology* (Vol. 3, pp. 39–80). New York: Academic Press.

Barnard, K. E., Hammond, M., Mitchell, S. K., Booth, C. L., Spitz, A., Snyder, C., & Elsas, T. (1985). Caring for high-risk infants and their families. In M. Green (Ed.), *The psychological aspects of the family* (pp. 244–259). Lexington, MA: Lexington Books.

Barnard, K. E., Magyary, D., Sumner, G. A., Booth, C. L., Mitchell, S. K., & Spieker, S. (1988). Prevention of parenting alterations for women with low social support. *Psychiatry, 51,* 248–253.

Beauchamp, D. E. (1985). Alcohol and the republic. *Journal of Drug Issues, 15,* 29–38.

Bee, H. L., Barnard, K. E., Dyres, S. J., Gray, C. A., Hammond, M. A., Spietz, A. L., Snyder, C., & Clark, B. (1982). Prediction of IQ and language skill from perinatal status, child performance, family characteristics, and mother-child interaction. *Child Development, 53,* 1134–1156.

Berman, P., & McLaughlin, M. W. (1978). *Federal programs sup-*

porting educational change: Vol. 8. Implementing and sustaining innovations. Santa Monica, CA: Rand Corporation.

Berrueta-Clement, J., Schweinhart, L., Barnett, W., Epstein, A., & Weikert, D. (1984). Changed lives: The effects of the Perry Preschool Program on youths through age 19. *Monographs of the High/Scope Educational Research Foundation, 8.*

Black, G. S. (1989). *Changing attitudes toward drug use: The first year effort of the Media-Advertising Partnership for a Drug-Free America, Inc.* Rochester, NY: Gordon S. Black Corporation.

Botvin, G. J. (1986). Substance abuse prevention research: Recent developments and future directions. *Journal of School Health, 56,* 369–374.

Botvin, G. J., Baker, E., Filazzola, A. D., & Botvin, E. M. (1990). A cognitive-behavioral approach to substance abuse prevention: One-year follow-up. *Addictive Behaviors, 15,* 47–63.

Bracht, N. (1990). *Health promotion at the community level.* Newbury Park, CA: Sage.

Bradley, R. H. (1987). Providing a stimulating and supportive home environment for young children. *Physical & Occupational Therapy in Pediatrics, 7*(4), 77–89.

Bronfenbrenner, U. (1986). Alienation and the four worlds of childhood. *Phi Delta Kappan, 67,* 430–436.

Brookover, W. B., Beamer, L., Efthim, H., Hathaway, D., Lezotte, L., Miller, S., Pasalacqua, J., & Tornatzky, L. (1982). *Creating effective schools: An inservice program for enhancing school learning climate and achievement.* Holmes Beach, FL: Learning.

Brophy, J., & Good, T. L. (1986). Teacher behavior and student achievement. In M. C. Wittrock (Ed.), *Handbook of research on training* (3rd ed., pp. 328–375). New York: Macmillan.

Bruner, J. (1981). The social context of language acquisition. *Language and Communication, 1,* 155–178.

Bukoski, W. J. (1986). School-based substance abuse prevention: A review of program research. In S. Griswold-Ezekoye, K. L. Kumpfer, & W. J. Bukoski (Eds.), *Childhood and chemical abuse* (pp. 95–115). New York: Haworth.

Caplan, M. Z., & Weissberg, R. P. (1989). Promoting social

competence in early adolescence: Developmental considerations. In B. H. Schneider, G. Attili, J. Nadel, & R. P. Weissberg (Eds.), *Social competence in developmental perspective* (pp. 371–385). Boston: Kluwer.

Carlaw, R. W., Mittelmark, M. B., Bracht, N., & Luepker, R. (1984). Organization for a community cardiovascular health program: Experiences from the Minnesota Heart Health Program. *Health Education Quarterly, 11,* 243–252.

Carnegie Council on Adolescent Development. (1989). *Turning points: Preparing American youth for the 21st century.* New York: Carnegie Council on Adolescent Development.

Carnine, D., Carnine, L., Karp, J., & Weisberg, P. (1988). Kindergarten for economically disadvantaged children: The direct instruction component. In C. Warger (Ed.), *A resource guide to public school early childhood programs* (pp. 73–78). Alexandria, VA: Association for Supervision and Curriculum Development.

Cartledge, G., & Milburn, J. F. (1986). *Teaching social skills to children* (2nd ed.). New York: Pergamon Press.

Cauce, A. M., Comer, J. P., & Schwartz, D. (1987). Long-term effects of a systems-oriented school prevention program. *American Journal of Orthopsychiatry, 57,* 127–131.

Chasnoff, I. J. (1991). *The perinatal influences of cocaine in the term newborn infant: A current look.* Report of the 100th Ross Conference on Pediatric Research. Columbus, OH: Ross Laboratories.

Chasnoff, I. J., Griffith, D. R., MacGregor, S., Dirkes, K., & Burns, K. A. (1989). Temporal patterns of cocaine use in pregnancy: Perinatal outcome. *Journal of the American Medical Association, 261,* 1741.

Chasnoff, I. J., Landress, H. J., & Barrett, M. E. (1990). The prevalence of illicit-drug or alcohol use during pregnancy and discrepancies in mandatory reporting in Pinellas County, Florida. *New England Journal of Medicine, 322,* 1202.

Children's Defense Fund. (1991). *The state of America's children.* Washington, DC: Children's Defense Fund.

Chubb, J. E. (1988). Why the current wave of school reform will fail. *Public Interest, 90,* 28–49.

Cicchette, D., & Toth, S. L. (1987). The application of a transactional risk model to intervention with multirisk maltreating families. *Zero to Three, 7*(5), 1-9.

Coie, J. D., Rabiner, D. L., & Lochman, J. E. (1989). Promoting peer relations in a school setting. In L. A. Bond & B. E. Compas (Eds.), *Primary prevention and promotion in the schools* (pp. 207-234). Newbury Park, CA: Sage.

Combs, M. L., & Slaby, D. A. (1977). Social-skills training with children. In B. B. Lahey & A. E. Kazdin (Eds.), *Advances in clinical child psychology* (Vol. 1, pp. 161-203). New York: Plenum.

Comer, J. P. (1980). *School power: Implications of an intervention project.* New York: Free Press.

Comer, J. P. (1988). Educating poor minority children. *Scientific American, 259*(5), 42-48.

Commins, W. (1987, May). *Institutionalization of mental health innovations: The case of elementary schools.* Paper presented at the Biennial Conference on Community Research and Action, Columbia, SC.

Connell, D. B., Turner, R. R., & Mason, E. F. (1985). Summary of the Findings of the School Health Education Evaluation: Health promotion effectiveness, implementation, and costs. *Journal of School Health, 55,* 316-323.

Cook, V. J., Howe, G. W., & Holliday, B. G. (1985). Community psychology for clinical child psychologists: Perspectives and roles. In S. I. Pfeiffer (Ed.), *Clinical child psychology: An introduction to theory, research, and practice* (pp. 331-364). Philadelphia: Grune & Stratton.

Cummings, C. (1983). *Managing to teach.* Edmonds, WA: Teaching, Inc.

Cummings, C. (1985). *Peering in on peers: Coaching teachers.* Edmonds, WA: Teaching, Inc.

Damon, W. (1988). *The moral child: Nurturing children's natural moral growth.* New York: Free Press.

DeFriese, G. H., Crossland, C. L., Pearson, C. E., & Sullivan, C. J. (1990). Comprehensive school health programs: Their current status and future prospects. *Journal of School Health, 60,* 127-128.

Didier, L. (1990, March). *Fred Meyer final report: Preparing for the Drug (Free) Years*. Salem, OR: Oregon Prevention Resource Center.

Doyle, W. (1986). Classroom organization and management. In M. E. Wittrock (Ed.), *Handbook of research on teaching* (3rd ed., pp. 392–431). New York: Macmillan.

Dryfoos, J. G. (1990). *Adolescents at risk: Prevalence and prevention*. New York: Oxford University Press.

Elder, J. P., Molgaard, C. A., & Gresham, L. (1988). Predictors of chewing tobacco and cigarette use in a multiethnic public school population. *Adolescence, 23,* 689–701.

Elias, M. J. (1990). The role of affect and social relationships in health behavior and school health curriculum instruction. *Journal of School Health, 60*(4), 157–163.

Elias, M. J., & Clabby, J. F. (1989). *Social decision-making skills: A curriculum guide for the elementary grades*. Rockville, MD: Aspen.

Elias, M. J., & Weissberg, R. P. (1990). School-based social competence promotion as a primary prevention strategy: A tale of two projects. In R. P. Lorion (Ed.), *Protecting the children: Strategies for optimizing emotional and behavioral development* (pp. 177–200). New York: Haworth Press.

Ellickson, P. L., & Bell, R. M. (1990). Drug prevention in junior high: A multi-site longitudinal test. *Science, 247,* 1299–1305.

Ellickson, P. L., & Robyn, A. E. (1987). *Toward more effective drug prevention programs*. Santa Monica, CA: Rand.

Estrada, P., Arsenio, W. F., Hess, R. D., & Holloway, S. D. (1987). Affective quality of the mother-child relationship: Longitudinal consequences for children's school-relevant cognitive functioning. *Developmental Psychology, 23,* 210–215.

Evans, R. I. (1976). Smoking in children: Developing a social psychological strategy of deterrence. *Preventive Medicine, 5,* 122–127.

Evans, R. I., Rozelle, R. M., Maxwell, S. E., Raines, B. E., Dill, C. A., & Guthrie, T. J. (1981). Social modeling films to deter smoking in adolescents: Results of a three-year investigation. *Journal of Applied Psychology, 66,* 399–414.

Farquhar, J. W. (1985). The Stanford five-city project: Design and methods. *American Journal of Epidemiology, 122,* 323–334.

Farquhar, J. W., Fortmann, S. P., Maccoby, N., Wood, P. D., Haskell, W. L., Taylor, C. B., Flora, J. A., Solomon, D. S., Rogers, T., Adler, E., Breitrose, P., & Weiner, L. (1984). The Stanford Five City Project: An overview. In J. D. Matarazzo, J. A. Herd, N. E. Miller, & S. M. Weiss (Eds.), *Behavioral health: A handbook of health enhancement and disease prevention* (pp. 1154–1165). New York: Wiley.

Flay, B. R. (1985). Psychosocial approaches to smoking prevention: A review of findings. *Health Psychology, 5,* 449–488.

Flay, B. R., Hansen, W. B., Johnson, C. A., Collins, L. M., Dent, C. W., Dwyer, K. M., Grossman, L., Hoskstein, G., Rauch, J., Sobel, J. L., Sobol, D. F., Sussman, S., & Ulene, A. (1987). Implementation effectiveness trial of a social influences smoking prevention program using schools and television. *Health Education Research, 2,* 385–400.

Flora, J. A., Maccoby, N., & Farquhar, J. W. (1989). Communication campaigns to prevent cardiovascular disease: The Stanford Community Studies. In R. E. Rice and C. K. Atkin (Eds.), *Public Communication Campaigns* (pp. 233–252). Newbury Park, CA: Sage.

Forman, S. G. (1982). Stress management for teachers: A cognitive-behavioral program. *Journal of School Psychology, 30,* 180–187.

Fraiberg, S. H. (1980). *Clinical studies in infant mental health: The first year of life.* New York: Basic Books.

Fraser, N. W., Hawkins, J. D., & Howard, M. O. (1988). Parent training for delinquency prevention: A review. *Child and Youth Services, 11,* 93–125.

Frymier, J., & Gansneder, B. (1989). The Phi Delta Kappa study of students at risk. *Phi Delta Kappan, 70,* 142–146.

Gilligan, C. (1987). Adolescent development reconsidered. In C. E. Irwin, Jr. (Ed.), *Adolescent social behavior and health* (New Directions for Child Development No. 37, pp. 63–92). San Francisco: Jossey-Bass.

Goodlad, J. (1984). *A place called school.* New York: McGraw-Hill.

Goodstadt, M. S. (1986). Alcohol education research and practice: A logical analysis of the two realities. *Journal of Drug Education, 16,* 349–365.

Goodstadt, M. S. (1989). Substance abuse curricula vs. school drug policies. *Journal of School Health, 59,* 246–250.

Gottfredson, D. C., Karweit, N. L., & Gottfredson, G. D. (1989). *Reducing disorderly behavior in middle schools.* Baltimore, MD: Center for Research on Elementary and Middle Schools.

Gottfredson, G. D. (1987, November). *Community influences on individual delinquency.* Paper presented at the annual meeting of the American Society of Criminology, Johns Hopkins University, Center for Social Organization of Schools, Baltimore, MD.

Gottfredson, G. D. (1988). *A workbook for your school improvement program.* Baltimore, MD: Johns Hopkins University, Center for Social Organization of Schools.

Gottfredson, G. D., & Gottfredson, D. C. (1989, June). *An approach to reducing risk through school system restructuring.* Paper presented for the Research Partnership Network, Johns Hopkins University, Baltimore, MD.

Grasmick, J. G., & Bryjak, G. J. (1980). The deterrent effect of perceived severity of punishment. *Social Forces, 59,* 471–491.

Greenberg, M. T., Cicchette, D., & Cummings, E. M. (Eds.). (1990). *Attachment in the preschool years.* Chicago: University of Chicago Press.

Greenspan, S., & Lourie, R. S. (1981). Developmental structuralist approach to the classification of adaptive and pathologic personality organization: Application to infancy and early childhood. *American Journal of Psychiatry, 138,* 6.

Grossman, M., Coate, D., & Arluck, G. M. (1987). Price sensitivity of alcoholic beverages in the United States: Youth alcohol consumption. In H. Holder (Ed.), *Advances in substance abuse: Behavioral and biological research: Supplement 1. Control issues in alcohol abuse prevention: Strategies for states and communities* (pp. 169–198). Greenwich, CT: JAI Press.

Gutkin, J. B., & Curtis, M. J. (1990). School-based consultation: Theory, research, and techniques. In J. B. Gutkin & C. R. Reynolds (Eds.), *The handbook of school psychology* (2nd ed., pp. 796–828). New York: Wiley.

Hansen, W. B., Johnson, C. A., Flay, B. R., Graham, J. W., & Sobel, J. (1988). Affective and social influences approaches to the prevention of multiple substance abuse among seventh-grade students: Results from Project SMART. *Preventive Medicine, 17,* 135–154.

Hartup, W. W. (1989). Social relationships and their developmental significance. *American Psychologist, 44,* 120–126.

Hawkins, J. D., & Catalano, R. F. (1990). Broadening the vision of education: Schools as health promoting environments. *Journal of School Health, 60,* 178–181.

Hawkins, J. D., Catalano, R. F., Jones, G., & Fine, D. (1987). Delinquency prevention through parent training: Results and issues from work in progress. In J. Wilson & G. Loury (Eds.), *From children to citizens: Families, schools, and delinquency prevention* (Vol. 3, pp. 186–204). New York: Springer-Verlag.

Hawkins, J. D., Catalano, R. F., & Kent, L. A. (1991). Combining broadcast media and parent education to prevent teenage drug abuse. In L. Donohew, H. E. Sypher, & W. J. Bukoski (Eds.), *Persuasive communication and drug abuse prevention* (pp. 283–294). Hillsdale, NJ: Erlbaum.

Hawkins, J. D., Catalano, R. F., & Miller, J. Y. (1992). Risk and protective factors for alcohol and other drug problems in adolescence and early adulthood: Implications for substance abuse prevention. *Psychological Bulletin, 112*(1), 64–105.

Hawkins, J. D., Doueck, H. J., & Lishner, D. M. (1988). Changing teaching practices in mainstream classrooms to improve bonding and behavior of low achievers. *American Educational Research Journal, 25,* 31–50.

Hawkins, J. D., & Lam, T. (1987). Teacher practices, social development, and delinquency. In J. D. Burchard & S. N. Burchard (Eds.), *Prevention of delinquent behavior* (pp. 241–274). Newbury Park, CA: Sage.

Hawkins, J. D., Von Cleve, E., & Catalano, R. F. (1991). Reducing early childhood aggression: Results of a primary prevention program. *Journal of the American Academy of Child and Adolescent Psychiatry, 30,* 208–217.

Hawley, R. A., Petersen, R. C., & Mason, M. C. (1986). *Curriculum for building drug-free schools.* Rockville, MD: American Council for Drug Education.

Hirschi, T. (1969). *Causes of delinquency.* Newbury Park, CA: Sage.

Hohmann, M., Banet, B., & Weikart, D. P. (1979). *Young children in ACTION: A manual for preschool educators: The cognitive oriented preschool curriculum.* Ypsilanti, MI: High/Scope Press.

Howard, J., Beckwith, L., Rodning, C., & Kropenske, V. (1989). The development of young children of substance-abusing parents: Insights from seven years of intervention and research. *Zero to Three, 9*(5), 8–12.

Howlin, P., & Rutter, M. (1987). The consequences of language delay for other aspects of development. In W. Yule & M. Rutter (Eds.), *Language development and language disorders* (pp. 271–294). Philadelphia: Lippincott.

Infant Health and Development Program. (1990). Enhancing the outcomes of low-birth-weight, premature infants. *Journal of the American Medical Association, 263,* 3035–3042.

Jacobs, D. R., Luepker, R. V., Mittelmark, M. B., Folsom, A. R., Pirie, P. L., Mascoili, S. R., Hannan, P. J., Pechacek, T. F., Bracht, N. F., Carlaw, R. W., Kline, F. G., & Blackburn, H. (1986). Community-wide prevention strategies: Evaluation design of the Minnesota Heart Health Program. *Journal of Chronic Diseases, 39,* 775–788.

Johnson, C. A., Pentz, M. A., Weber, M. D., Dwyer, J. H., Baer, N. A., MacKinnon, D. P., Hansen, W. B., & Flay, B. R. (1989). Relative effectiveness of comprehensive community programming for drug abuse prevention with high-risk and low-risk adolescents. *Journal of Consulting and Clinical Psychology, 58,* 447–456.

Johnson, D. W., & Johnson, R. T. (1980). Effects of cooperative, competitive, and individualistic learning experiences on cross-ethnic interaction and friendships. *Journal of Social Psychology, 118,* 47–58.

Johnston, L. D., O'Malley, P. M., & Bachman, J. G. (1991). *Drug use among American high school seniors, college students, and young adults, 1975–1990: Vol. 1. High school seniors.* Washington, DC: National Institute on Drug Abuse.

Jones, B. (1988). Toward redefining models of curriculum and instruction for students at risk. In B. Presseisen (Ed.), *At-risk students and thinking: Perspectives from research* (pp. 76–103).

Washington, DC: National Education Association/Research for Better Schools.

Kandel, D., Simcha-Fagan, O., & Davis, M. (1986). Risk factors for delinquency and illicit drug use from adolescence to young adulthood. *Journal of Drug Issues, 16,* 67–90.

Kang, R., Rollolazo, M., Yoshihara, K., & Thibodeaux, B. Z. (1989). *Prenatal and postpartum nursing protocols.* Supported by a grant from the U.S. Public Health Service, Division of Maternal and Child Health, Grant No. MCJ-533462 to K. Barnard, University of Washington. Revision by K. C. Carr available through Washington State Plan for Nursing, DSHS Parent-Child Health Services Contract with the University of Washington School of Nursing, WJ-10, Seattle, Washington.

Karweit, N. L. (1989a). Effective kindergarten programs and practices for students at risk. In R. E. Slavin, N. L. Karweit, & N. A. Madden (Eds.), *Effective programs for students at risk* (pp. 103–142). Needham Heights, MA: Allyn and Bacon.

Karweit, N. L. (1989b). *The effects of a story reading program on the vocabulary and story comprehension skills of disadvantaged prekindergarten and kindergarten students* (CREMS Report No. 39). Baltimore, MD: Johns Hopkins University, Center for Research on Elementary and Middle Schools.

Karweit, N. L. (1989c). Effective preschool programs for students at risk. In R. E. Slavin, N. L. Karweit, & N. A. Madden (Eds.), *Effective programs for students at risk* (pp. 75–102). Needham Heights, MA: Allyn and Bacon.

Kendall, P. C. (1991). Guiding theory for therapy with children and adolescents. In P. C. Kendall (Ed.), *Child and adolescent therapy: Cognitive-behavioral procedures* (pp. 3–22). New York: Guilford Press.

Kendall, P. C., & Broswell, L. (1982). Cognitive-behavioral self-control therapy for children: A components analysis. *Journal of Consulting and Clinical Psychology, 50,* 672–689.

Kendall, P. C., Reber, M., McLeer, S., Epps, J., & Ronan, K. (1990). Cognitive-behavioral treatment of conduct-disordered children. *Cognitive Therapy and Research, 14,* 279–297.

Klepp, K.-I., Halper, A., & Perry, C. L. (1986). The efficacy of peer leaders in drug abuse prevention. *Journal of School Health, 56*(9), 407–411.

Larner, M., & Halpern, R. (1987). Lay home visiting programs: Strengths, tensions, and challenges. *Zero to Three, 8,* 1–7.

Lazar, I., Darlington, R., Murray, H., Royce, J., & Snipper, A. (1982). Lasting effects of early education. *Monographs of the Society for Research in Child Development, 47,* 1–151.

Levenstein, P., O'Hara, J., & Madden, J. (1983). The Mother-Child Home Program of the Verbal Interaction Project. In Consortium for Longitudinal Studies, *As the twig is bent: Lasting effects of preschool programs* (pp. 237–264). Hillsdale, NJ: Erlbaum.

Little, J. W. (1982). Norms of collegiality and experimentation: Workplace conditions of school success. *American Education Research Journal, 19,* 32–40.

Markman, H. J., Duncan, W., Storaalski, R. D., & Howes, P. W. (1987). The prediction and prevention of marital distress: A longitudinal investigation in understanding major mental disorder. In K. Hahlweg & M. Goldstein (Eds.), *Understanding major mental disorder: The contribution of family interaction research* (pp. 266–289). New York: Family Process Press.

Markman, H. J., & Kadushin, F. S. (1986). Preventive effects of Lamaze training for first time parents: A short-term longitudinal study. *Journal of Consulting and Clinical Psychology, 54*(6), 872–874.

Mason, J. A., & Allen, J. (1986). A review of emergent literacy with implications for research and practice in reading. In E. Rothkopf (Ed.), *Review of research in education in America* (Vol. 13, pp. 3–47). Washington, DC: American Educational Research Association.

McAlister, A. L., Perry, C. L., Killen, J., Slinkard, L. A., & Maccoby, N. (1980). Pilot study of smoking, alcohol, and drug abuse prevention. *American Journal of Public Health, 70,* 719–721.

McCormick, C., & Mason, J. (1987). Intervention procedures for increasing preschool children's interest in and knowledge about reading. In W. H. Teale and E. Sulzby (Eds.), *Emer-*

gent literacy: Writing and reading (pp. 90–115). Norwood, NJ: Ablex.

McMahon, E. T., & Taylor, P. A. (1990). *Citizens' action handbook on alcohol and tobacco billboard advertising.* Washington, DC: Center for Science in the Public Interest.

McMahon, R. J., & Forehand, R. (1984). Parent training for the noncompliant child: Treatment outcome, generalization, and adjunctive therapy procedures. In R. F. Dangel & R. A. Polster (Eds.), *Parent training: Foundations of research and practice* (pp. 298–328). New York: Guilford Press.

Mercer, R. T. (1990). *Parents at risk.* New York: Springer.

Merriam, J. E. (1989). National media coverage of drug issues: 1983–1987. In P. J. Shoemaker (Ed.), *Communications campaigns about drugs: Government, media, and the public* (pp. 21–28). Hillsdale, NJ: Erlbaum.

Miller, C. A. (1991). *Maternal health and infant survival.* Arlington, VA: National Center for Clinical Infant Programs.

Mirman, J., Swartz, R., & Barell, J. (1988). Strategies to help teachers empower at-risk students. In B. Presseisen (Ed.), *At-risk students and thinking: Perspectives from research* (pp. 138–156). Washington, DC: National Education Association/Research for Better Schools.

Morisset, C. E., Barnard, K. E., Greenberg, M. T., Booth, C. L., & Spieker, S. J. (1990). Environmental influences on early language development: The context of social risk. *Development and Psychopathology, 2,* 127–149.

Mosher, J. F. (1985). Alcohol policy and the nation's youth. *Journal of Public Health Policy, 6,* 295–299.

Mosher, J. F., & Jernigan, D. H. (1989). New directions in alcohol policy. *Annual Review of Public Health, 10,* 245–279.

Moskowitz, J. M. (1983). Preventing adolescent substance abuse through drug education. In T. J. Glynn, C. G. Leukefeld, & J. P. Ludford (Eds.), *Preventing adolescent drug abuse: Intervention strategies* (NIDA Research Monograph No. 47, pp. 233–249). Washington, DC: U.S. Government Printing Office.

Moskowitz, J. M. (1989). The primary prevention of alcohol problems: A critical review of the research literature. *Journal of Studies on Alcohol, 50,* 54–88.

Murray, D. M., Davis-Hearn, M., Goldman, A. I., Pirie, P., & Luepker, R. V. (1988). Four- and five-year follow-up results from four seventh-grade smoking prevention strategies. *Journal of Behavioral Medicine, 11,* 395–405.

Murray, D. M., Pirie, P., Luepker, R. V., & Pallonen, U. (1989). Five- and six-year follow-up results from four seventh-grade smoking prevention strategies. *Journal of Behavioral Medicine, 12,* 207–218.

Murray, D. M., Richards, P. S., Luepker, R. V., & Johnson, C. A. (1987). The prevention of cigarette smoking in children: Two- and three-year follow-up comparisons of four prevention strategies. *Journal of Behavioral Medicine, 10,* 595–611.

Musick, J. S., Bernstein, V., Percansky, C., & Stott, F. M. (1987). A chain of enablement: Using community-based programs to strengthen relationships between teen parents and their infants. *Zero to Three, 8*(2), 1–6.

National Commission on Excellence in Education. (1983). *A nation at risk: The imperative for educational reform. A report to the nation and the Secretary of Education, U.S. Department of Education.* Washington, DC: U.S. Government Printing Office.

National Governors' Association Committee on Human Resources and Center for Policy Research. (1987). *Focus on the first sixty months: A handbook of promising prevention programs for children zero to five years of age.* Washington, DC: National Governors' Association.

National Institute of Education. (1985). *Becoming a nation of readers* (Report of the Commission on Reading). Washington, DC: U.S. Department of Education, National Institute of Education.

Newcomb, M. D., Maddahian, E., & Bentler, P. M. (1986). Risk factors for drug use among adolescents: Concurrent and longitudinal analyses. *American Journal of Public Health, 76,* 525–530.

O'Donnell, J. A., Hawkins, J. D., Catalano, R. F., Abbott, R. D., & Day, L. E. (1991). *Preventing school failure, drug use, and delinquency among low-income children: Effects of a long-term prevention project in elementary schools.* Manuscript submitted for publication.

Office of National Drug Control Policy. (1990). *Leading drug indicators*. Washington, DC: Office of National Drug Control Policy, Executive Office of the President.

Olds, D. L., Henderson, C. R., Chamberlin, R., & Tatelbaum, R. (1986). Preventing child abuse and neglect: A randomized trial of nurse home visitation. *Pediatrics, 78*(1), 65–78.

Palincsar, A., & Brown, A. (1985). Reciprocal teaching: Activities to promote "reading with your mind." In T. Harris & E. Cooper (Eds.), *Reading, thinking, and concept development: Strategies for the classroom* (pp. 47–160). New York: College Entrance Examination Board.

Patterson, G. R. (1986). Performance models for antisocial boys. *American Psychologist, 41*, 432–444.

Patterson, G. R., Chamberlain, P., & Reid, J. B. (1982). A comparative evaluation of a parent training program. *Behavior Therapy, 13*, 638–650.

Pentz, M. A., Brannon, B. R., Charlin, V. L., Barrett, E. J., MacKinnon, D. P., & Flay, B. R. (1989). The power of policy: The relationship of smoking policy to adolescent smoking. *American Journal of Public Health, 79*, 857–862.

Pentz, M. A., Dwyer, J. H., MacKinnon, D. P., Flay, B. R., Hansen, W. B., Wang, E. Y. I., & Johnson, C. A. (1989). A multicommunity trial for primary prevention of adolescent drug abuse. *Journal of the American Medical Association, 261*, 3259–3266.

Perry, C. L., Kelder, S. H., & Komro, K. (in press). *The social world of adolescents: Family, peers, schools, and culture*. Washington, DC: Carnegie Council on Adolescents, Carnegie Corporation.

Perry, C. L., Klepp, K.-I., & Sillers, C. (1989). Community-wide strategies for cardiovascular health: The Minnesota Heart Health Program youth program. *Health Education and Research, 4*(1), 87–101.

Perry, C. L., Pirie, P., Holder, W., Halper, A., & Dudovitz, B. (1990). Parent involvement in cigarette smoking prevention: Two pilot evaluations of the Unpuffables Program. *Journal of School Health, 60*, 443–447.

Polich, J. M., Ellickson, P. L., Reuter, P., & Kahan, J. P. (1984). *Strategies for controlling adolescent drug use*. Santa Monica, CA: Rand.

Postman, N., Nystrom, C., Strate, L., & Weingartner, C. (1988). *Miffs, men, and beer: An analysis of beer commercials on broadcast television.* Washington, DC: AAA Foundation for Traffic Safety.

Presseisen, B. Z. (1988). Teaching thinking and at-risk students: Defining a population. In B. Z. Presseisen (Ed.), *At-risk students and thinking: Perspectives from research* (pp. 19–37). Washington, DC: National Education Association/Research for Better Schools.

Public Health Service Expert Panel on the Content of Prenatal Care. (1989). *Caring for our future: The content of prenatal care.* Washington, DC: Public Health Service, Department of Health and Human Services.

Ramey, C. T., Bryant, D. M., Wasik, B. H., Sparling, J. J., Fendt, K. H., & LaVange, L. M. (in press). The Infant Health and Development Program for low birthweight, premature infants: program elements, family participation, and child intelligence. *Pediatrics.*

Ramey, C. T., Farran, D. D., & Campbell, F. (1978). Predicting IQ from mother-infant interaction. *Child Development, 50,* 804–814.

Rice, D. P., Kelman, S., Miller, L. S., & Dunmeyer, S. (1990). *The economic costs of alcohol and drug abuse and mental illness* (Contract No. 283-87-0007). San Francisco: Office of Financing and Coverage Policy of the Alcohol, Drug Abuse, and Mental Health Administration; U.S. Department of Health and Human Services.

Robins, L. N., & Przybeck, T. R. (1985). Age of onset of drug use as a factor in drug and other disorders. In C. L. Jones & R. J. Battjes (Eds.), *Etiology of drug abuse: Implications for prevention* (pp. 178–192) (NIDA Research Monograph No. 56, DHHS Publication No. ADM 85-1335). Washington, DC: U.S. Government Printing Office.

Rosenshine, B. V. (1986, April). Synthesis of research on explicit teaching. *Educational Leadership,* pp. 60–69.

Rotheram, M. J. (1982a). Social skills training for underachievers, disruptive, and exceptional children. *Psychology in the Schools, 19,* 532–539.

Rotheram, M. J. (1982b). Variations in children's assertiveness due to training assertion level. *Journal of Community Psychology, 10,* 228–236.

Rotheram, M. J. (1987). Children's social and academic competence. *Journal of Educational Research, 80*(4), 206–211.

Rutter, M. (1985). Resilience in the face of adversity: Protective factors and resistance to psychiatric disturbance. *British Journal of Psychiatry, 147,* 598–611.

Rutter, M. (1987). Temperament, personality, and personality disorder. *British Journal of Psychiatry, 150,* 443–458.

Sameroff, A. J., & Emde, R. N. (Eds.). (1990). *Relationship disturbances in early childhood: A developmental approach.* New York: Basic Books.

Sameroff, A. J., & Seifer, R. (1983). Familial risk and child competence. *Child Development, 54,* 1254–1268.

Schinke, S. P., Bebel, M. Y., Orlandi, M. A., & Botvin, G. J. (1988). Prevention strategies for vulnerable pupils: School social work practices to prevent substance abuse. *Urban Education, 22,* 510–519.

Schinke, S. P., Botvin, G. J., Trimble, J. E., Orlandi, M. A., Gilchrist, L. D., & Locklear, V. S. (1988). Preventing substance abuse among American-Indian adolescents: A bicultural competence skills approach. *Journal of Counseling Psychology, 35,* 87–90.

Schorr, L. (1988). *Within our reach: Breaking the cycle of disadvantage.* Garden City, NY: Anchor Press.

Shanok, R. S. (1990). Parenthood: A process marking identity and intimacy capacities. *Zero to Three, 9*(2), 1–8.

Shedler, J., & Block, J. (1990). Adolescent drug use and psychological health: A longitudinal inquiry. *American Psychologist, 45,* 612–630.

Simcha-Fagan, O., Gersten, J. C., & Langner, T. (1986). Early precursors and concurrent correlates of illicit drug use in adolescents. *Journal of Drug Issues, 16,* 7–28.

Slavin, R. E. (1979). Effects of biracial learning teams on cross-racial friendships. *Journal of Education Psychology, 71,* 381–387.

Slavin, R. E. (1983). When does cooperative learning increase student achievement? *Psychological Bulletin, 94,* 429–445.

Slavin, R. E. (1990). *Cooperative learning theory, research, and practice*. Englewood Cliffs, NJ: Prentice Hall.

Spieker, S. J., & Booth, C. L. (1988). Maternal antecedents of attachment quality. In J. Belsky & T. Nezworski (Eds.), *Clinical implications of attachment* (pp. 95–134). Hillsdale, NJ: Erlbaum.

Spitzer, A., Webster-Stratton, C., & Hollinsworth, T. (1991). Coping with conduct-problem children: Parents gaining knowledge and control. *Journal of Clinical Child Psychology, 20,* 413–427.

Spivack, G., Platt, J., & Shure, M. (1976). *The problem-solving approach to adjustment: A guide to research and intervention*. San Francisco: Jossey-Bass.

Spivack, G., & Shure, M. B. (1989). Interpersonal Cognitive Problem Solving (ICPS): A competence-building primary prevention program. *Prevention in the Human Services, 6,* 151–178.

Stallings, J. A., & Stipek, D. (1986). Research on early childhood and elementary school teaching programs. In M. C. Wittrock (Ed.), *Handbook of research on teaching.* (3rd ed., pp. 727–753). New York: Macmillan.

Stephens, T. M. (1978). *Social skills in the classroom*. Columbus, OH: Cedars Press.

Streissguth, A. P., Aase, J. M., Sterling, K. C., Randels, S. P., LaDue, R. A., & Smith, D. F. (1991). Fetal alcohol syndrome in adolescents and adults. *Journal of the American Medical Association, 265,* 1961–1967.

Stroufe, A. (1983). Infant-caregiver attachment and patterns of adaptation in preschool: The roots of maladaptation and competence. In M. Perlmutter (Ed.), *Minnesota Symposia on Child Psychology* (Vol. 16, pp. 44–85). Hillsdale, NJ: Erlbaum.

Tableman, B., & Katzenmeyer, M. (1985). *Infant mental health services: A newborn screener*. Lansing: Michigan Department of Mental Health.

Tobler, N. S. (1986). Meta-analysis of 143 adolescent drug prevention programs: Quantitative outcome results of program participants compared to a control or comparison group. *Journal of Drug Issues, 16,* 537–567.

Tronick, E. (1989). Emotions and emotional communication in infancy. *American Psychologist, 44,* 112–119.

U.S. General Accounting Office (GAO). (1990). *Home visiting:*

A promising early intervention strategy for at-risk families. Washington, DC: U.S. General Accounting Office.

U.S. Surgeon General. (1988). *The health consequences of smoking: Nicotine addiction. A report of the Surgeon General.* Rockville, MD: U.S. Department of Health and Human Services.

Vartiainen, E., Pallonen, U., McAlister, A., Koskela, K., & Puska, P. (1983). Effect of two years of educational intervention on adolescent smoking in the North Karelia Youth Project. *Bulletin of the World Health Organization, 61,* 529–532.

Vartiainen, E., Pallonen, U., McAlister, A., Koskela, K., & Puska, P. (1986). Four-year follow-up results of the smoking prevention program in the North Karelia Youth Project. *Preventive Medicine, 15,* 692–698.

Vartiainen, E., Pallonen, U., McAlister, A., & Puska, P. (1990). Eight-year follow-up results of an adolescent smoking prevention program: The North Karelia Youth Project. *American Journal of Public Health, 80,* 78–79.

Walberg, H. J. (1986). Synthesis of research on teaching. In M. C. Wittrock (Ed.), *Handbook of research on teaching* (3rd ed., pp. 214–229). New York: Macmillan.

Walberg, H. J. (1988, March). Synthesis of research on time and learning. *Educational Leadership,* pp. 76–85.

Warger, C. (Ed.). (1988). *A resource guide to public school early childhood programs.* Alexandria, VA: Association for Supervision and Curriculum Development.

Webster-Stratton, C. (1982). The long-term effects of a videotape modeling parent-training program: Comparison of immediate and 1-year follow-up results. *Behavior Therapy, 13,* 702–714.

Webster-Stratton, C. (1984). Randomized trial of two parent-training programs for families with conduct-disordered children. *Journal of Counseling and Clinical Psychology, 52,* 666–678.

Webster-Stratton, C. (1989). Systematic comparison of consumer satisfaction of three cost-effective parent training programs for conduct-problem children. *Behavior Therapy, 20,* 103–115.

Webster-Stratton, C., Kolpacoff, M., & Hollinsworth, T. (1988). Self-administered videotape therapy for families with conduct-problem children: Comparison with two cost-effective treatments and a control group. *Journal of Consulting and Clinical Psychology, 56,* 558–566.

Webster-Stratton, C., Kolpacoff, M., & Hollinsworth, T. (1989). The long-term effectiveness and clinical significance of three cost-effective training programs for families with conduct-problem children. *Journal of Consulting and Clinical Psychology, 57,* 550–553.

Weinraub, M., & Wolf, B. (1983). Effects of stress and social supports on mother-child interactions in single and two-parent families. *Child Development, 54,* 1297–1311.

Weiss, H. B. (1988). Family support and education programs: Working through ecological theories of human development. In H. B. Weiss & F. H. Jacobs (Eds.), *Evaluating family programs* (pp. 3–36). New York: de Gruyter.

Weissberg, R. P., Caplan, M. Z., & Sivo, P. J. (1989). A new conceptual framework for establishing school-based social competence promotion programs. In L. A. Bond & B. E. Compas (Eds.), *Primary prevention and promotion in the schools* (pp. 177–200). Newbury Park, CA: Sage.

Weissberg, R. P., Gesten, E. L., Carnrike, C. L., Toro, P. A., Rapkin, B. D., Davidson, E., & Cowen, E. L. (1981). Social problem-solving skills training: A competence building intervention with second- to fourth-grade children. *American Journal of Community Psychology, 9,* 411–423.

Weston, D. R., Ivins, B., Zuckerman, B., Jones, C. J., & Lopez, R. (1990). Drug exposed babies: Research and clinical issues. *Zero to Three, 9*(5), 1–7.

Williams, B. C., & Miller, C. A. (1991). *Preventive health care for young children: Findings from a 10-country study and directions for United States policy.* Arlington, VA: National Center for Clinical Infant Programs.

Winsten, J. A., & DeJong, W. (1989). *Recommendations for future mass media campaigns to prevent preteen and adolescent substance abuse.* Cambridge, MA: Harvard School of Public Health, Center for Health Communication.

Zuckerman, B., Frank, D. A., Hingson, R., Amaro, H., Levenson, S. M., Kayne, H., Parker, S., Vinci, R., Aboague, K., & Fried, L. E. (1989). Effects of maternal marijuana and cocaine use on fetal growth. *New England Journal of Medicine, 320,* 762–768.

Name Index

233

Subject Index

A

Academic failure: and early childhood education, 69–70; and instructional improvement, 115, 123–124; and prenatal and infancy programs, 54, 55; risk from, 11–12; strategy selection for, 45, 46

Acceptability, and funding success, 202–204

Accountability, and drug use policies, 157, 160, 163, 165

Active learning: in early childhood, 74; and instructional improvement, 117

Addictions, in pregnancy, 57, 63, 64

Advertising: agency for, 183; and drug use policies, 158, 162–163; programming distinct from, 183–184

African-Americans: advertising targeted to, 158; first-grade retention rate for, 69

Aggressiveness: and early childhood education, 70; risk from early, 11

Aid to Families with Dependent Children (AFDC), 198

AIDS epidemic, and prevention curricula, 142

Alcohol, community and school policies on, 149–169

Alcohol, Drug Abuse, and Mental Health Administration, 3

Alcoholism in family: and parent training, 86; risk from, 11

Alienation, risk from, 12

American Council for Drug Education, 166, 168

Antisocial behavior, risk from, 12

Assessment: of community risks, 30–32; for drug use policies, 162–163; for prevention curricula, 143–144

Attachment: for bonding, 14; and early childhood education, 73; and

239